ABOUT WHAT I KNOW

THE BUDDHA'S PROCESS OF SPIRITUAL CULTIVATION, REALIZATION AND ENLIGHTENMENT

A TREATISE AND COMMENTARIES IN QUESTION AND ANSWER FORMAT

THÍCH THÔNG TRIỆT

Second edition

Buddhist calendar year: 2561 – Calendar Year: 2017

SUNYATA FOUNDATION
Perris, California

Copyright © 2014 by Thich Thong Triet (Vietnamese original)
Copyright © 2016 by Thich Thong Triet (English translation)

Materials contained in this book may be reproduced without permission from the publisher provided that you charge no fees of any kind. Otherwise, all rights reserved.

Translated from the Vietnamese by Thông Như and Sunyata Meditation students
Cover design by Tuệ Nguyên

First edition published 2016
Second edition published 2017

Printed in the United States of America

ISBN 978-0-9986920-0-5 (paper)

Published by Sunyata Foundation
18525 Frantz Road
Perris, California 92570
www.sunyatameditation.org

Library of Congress Control Number: 2017932741

CONTENTS

Contents i
Dedication iii
Acknowledgements v
Preface vii

INTRODUCTION 1
About This Book 2
Book Summary 8
Chapter Summaries 12

CHAPTER I - THE SUPREME BEING AND HIS MOTIVATIONS 25
1 In Search Of The Light Of The Buddha's Teaching On Meditation 26
2 The Historical Buddha 31
3 The Supreme Being 37

CHAPTER II - THE INVALUABLE EXPERIENCE 55
1 The First Journey: Leaving Home To Seek The Spiritual Path .. 56
2 Searching For Spiritual Teachers 62
3 The Second Journey: Self-Mortification 72

CHAPTER III - THE DECISIVE STAGE 103
1 The Third Journey: The Middle Path And The Process Of Spiritual Realization 104
2 Spiritual Realization 150

CHAPTER IV - THE ENLIGHTENMENT PROCESS 165
1 The Foundations Of The Buddha's Enlightenment 166
2 The Essence Of The Buddha's Enlightenment 171
3 The Significance Of The Buddha's Enlightenment 193
4 Conclusion 209

NOTES 211
Notes to the Introduction 212
Notes to Chapter I 215

Notes to Chapter II 241
Notes to Chapter III 253
Notes to Chapter IV 263

DEDICATION

This book is dedicated to all meditation students who have attended the Śūnyatā Meditation courses in and outside the United States of America:

1. **USA:** *Southern California, San Jose, Sacramento (California); Florida; Houston (Texas); Portland (Oregon); Seattle (Washington State); Virginia; Washington D.C.;*

2. **France:** *Paris, Toulouse;*

3. **Germany:** *Stuttgart, Frankfurt, Krefeld;*

4. **Canada:** *Toronto, Ottawa, Montreal;*

5. **Switzerland:** *Lausanne;*

6. **Australia:** *Sydney, Adelaide, Melbourne.*

ACKNOWLEDGEMENTS

For the Vietnamese original version

This book entitled *The Buddha's Process of Spiritual Cultivation, Realization and Enlightenment - A Treatise and Commentaries in Question and Answer Format* has been published owing to favorable causal conditions, especially the generous contributions from meditation students in France, Germany, Australia, Canada, Switzerland and the United States of America.

I would like to express special thanks to the following people:

- Bhikkhuni Zen Master Triệt Như for proof reading and reviewing the final document before printing;

- Ms. Triệt Huệ, Ms. Thanh Nguyệt, Ms. Diệu Nhân for typing the manuscript;

- Mr. Tuệ Nguyên for layout and photos;

- Mr. Nguyên Hạnh for designing the book cover;

- Ms. Triệt Huệ, Mr. Không Giới and Ms. Thuần Chánh Tín for printing and distribution;

- Bhikkhuni Ý Như and Ms. Diệu Nhân (Sacramento, CA), Ms. Minh Ngộ and Ms. Triệt Huệ (Southern California), Ms. Thuần Tuệ and Ms. Minh Tuyết (Houston) for organizing the accommodation and catering at the nominated practice communities.

To all Buddhists and meditation students who have directly or indirectly provided encouragement and assistance, including help in regard to Buddhist suttas and commentaries and scientific publications, I would like to transfer the merits that you have garnered by supporting the dhamma. May all Buddhas from the ten directions, in their compassion, bestow unto you their blessing and protection.

Thích Thông Triệt
Riverside, California
Buddhist calendar year 2558 – Calendar year 2014

For the English version

I would like to express my thanks to the following meditation students who have contributed to this English version of the book:

- Mr. Thông Như for performing, and Mr. Như Lưu for editing, the translation into English;

- Ms. Hoàng Liên and Ms. Ngọc Huyền for checking the translation work;

- Dr. Jenny Barnett and Bhikkhu Thích Không Triệt for editing the English text after it had been translated;

- Mr. Tuệ Nguyên and Ms. Hoàng Liên for the design and content of the book cover;

- Mr. Như Lưu for the layout of the book interior;

- Mr. Tuệ Chiếu, Mr. Tuệ Huy, Ms. Như Tịnh, and Mr. Tuệ Quán for providing comments and general advice as part of their membership of the translation committee.

Thích Thông Triệt
Riverside, California
Buddhist calendar year 2561 – Calendar year 2017

PREFACE

The Buddha's Process of Spiritual Cultivation, Realization and Enlightenment - A Treatise and Commentaries in Question and Answer Format

Reasons for this book

I published a book entitled "The Buddha's Process of Spiritual Cultivation and Realization" in 1999 and reprinted it in 2007 as part of a 4-book series entitled "Understanding and Practice of Buddhist Meditation". I am now removing "The Buddha's Process of Spiritual Cultivation and Realization" from the series and having it stand on its own, under a new title: "The Buddha's Process of Spiritual Cultivation, Realization and Enlightenment - A Treatise and Commentaries in Question and Answer Format".

From 2007 to 2010, following a series of brain imaging studies conducted at the University of Tuebingen, Germany and after attending the OHBM (Organization for Human Brain Imaging) 16th Conference in Barcelona, Spain and the 17th Conference in Quebec City, Canada, I had the answer to the question that had preoccupied me since 1982: the mind that is malleable, pure, unblemished, wieldy and beyond word-thought is a function of the precuneus. This state of mind is equivalent to what Buddhist texts call the Suchness-Mind.

Indeed, other terms used by the Buddha such as *Tathāgata* (meaning thus gone/thus come), the Unborn, the Higher Wisdom, *Nibbāna* (or Nirvāṇa in Sanskrit), or the Pure Nature all refer to the function of the precuneus. The precuneus is located in the parietal lobe of the cerebral cortex and has been described by neuroscientists as the core of the brain.

I have added a study of the "Buddha's Process of Enlightenment" to shed further light on "the Buddha's Process of Spiritual Cultivation and Realization". This has resulted in this new book, entitled: "The Buddha's Process of Spiritual Cultivation, Realization and Enlightenment: A Treatise and Commentaries in Question and Answer Format".

Objectives

I have four objectives in writing this book:

1. To explain and comment on the key points of the Buddha's process of spiritual cultivation and realization through the four stages of samādhi (stillness of mind) meditation.
2. To explain and comment on the process by which the Buddha attained enlightenment.
3. To draw a parallel with the suttas in which the Buddha taught his disciples the methods to achieve the four samādhi stages and the ultimate liberation he had himself attained.
4. To give meditation students directions for practice using today's language.

I hope that this book will be of assistance to all those who wish to gain a deeper understanding of Buddhist meditation through the study of Early Buddhist texts.

Thích Thông Triệt
Śūnyatā Meditation Center, Perris, California
May 2014

INTRODUCTION

ABOUT THIS BOOK

References

This book draws materials primarily from the following sources:

1. The Nikāyas and Āgamas, reference texts of the Southern and Northern Schools of Buddhism respectively.
2. The Suttas of the Developmental School of Buddhism.
3. Commentaries on Buddhism written in English and Vietnamese.

When providing an explanation of the more technical terms used in Buddhist and Zen Buddhist texts, I have relied on a number of Pāli-English and Sanskrit-English dictionaries, Chinese - Vietnamese Buddhist dictionaries, a Zen and Buddhist dictionary with Pāli, Sanskrit and English annotations and my own unpublished Buddhist Encyclopedic Dictionary.

All the above references are mentioned at the end of each chapter.

Reasons for this book

One day during my seven years of "unsolicited meditation retreat" from 1975 to 1982, I felt I was at a dead end and was in utter despair because I had been practicing strenuously without ever experiencing samādhi. On the contrary, my mind continued to be carried away by wandering thoughts. In this state of utter impasse, I took a ball pen and wrote a series of "no" words on a piece of paper: *no meditation, no contemplation, no tranquility, no stillness, no abiding, no no, no leaving, no without, no extinguishing, no collecting, no nothingness, no, no, no, no!*

I made a strong stroke of the ball pen under the last "no" word, and as I looked up, my arm swung over my head, I immediately had the answer that had eluded me for so long, that is: "Samādhi is achieved when there is *no verbal chattering in the mind*!". I laughed out loud with joy! At that moment I realized that for too long I had been caught in the academic and complicated terminology of Zen Buddhist commentary texts. I was confused by the Zen terminology! Once I stripped away the academic and complicated terminology and just *stopped the verbal chattering* in my mind, I was able to step into the clear, empty and all-enveloping awareness of the wordless awareness mind! Four lines of verses immediately sprang into my mind:

I have finished with worldly matters
My mind is serene like the clouds over the forest
There is nothing that needs to be said
Thoughts cease, words stop, mind is empty!

I knew that this was a spiritual realization.

Once I identified the reason for my realization, I made a vow: when I recover my freedom, I will study the Pāli texts of Early Buddhism and will present the process by which the Buddha **practiced, attained his spiritual realization and then attained his enlightenment** to shed light on Buddhist meditation.

In 1992, once causal conditions were met, I migrated to the USA under the Humanitarian Operation program. In October 1994, the Most Venerable Thích Thanh Từ visited me in Oregon, officially certified my Sunyata Meditation Centre and authorized me to conduct Fundamental

Meditation courses there. At the beginning of 1995, causal conditions were met and I conducted the first Fundamental Meditation course in Beaverton, Oregon. I based the course on a development of the method "Be Aware of Your Wandering Thoughts but Do Not Follow Them" that the Most Venerable had established in his book "Vietnamese Zen Buddhism in the Late 20th Century".

In 1997, I conducted my third Fundamental Meditation course in Corona, California and introduced the concept of "Using the Buddha as the Source". This means that, as the basis of my meditation teaching, I used the Buddhist Pāli suttas and draw on two processes (1) how the Buddha practiced and attained his spiritual realization and (2) how the Buddha attained his full enlightenment. These processes represent the essence of Buddhist meditation that has always been based on **awareness** (*pajānati* in Pāli), as in "to be aware of" or "to know clearly". The meditation practitioner must follow these processes if s/he wishes to reach the destination. The Buddha himself experienced these processes. If we follow his teaching, we will in turn eventually reach the same destination.

I have discussed the first process in three chapters. The first two chapters are commentaries that help the meditation student follow closely the journey taken by the Buddha. In particular, in Chapter III, I have provided a detailed analysis of the four samādhi meditation stages that the Buddha experienced on his journey to spiritual realization. It is noted that this process is not commemorated at Bodh Gaya.

The second process is the most important process in the history of Buddhism. It is the process by which the Buddha attained **full enlightenment**, when he realized the Law of

INTRODUCTION 5

Dependent Origination and the Law of Dependently Arisen Phenomena.

Following this realization, the Buddha was proclaimed as the Supreme Full Enlightened One (*Anuttara-sammā-sambhodi* in Pāli). At Bodh Gaya, there are markings commemorating the seven weeks of this process. The fourth week is represented by a roofless house, called the "Jewel House", marking the place where the Buddha realized the Law of Dependent Origination and the Law of Dependently Arisen Phenomena.

To give a clear account of this process of enlightenment, I will refer step by step to the relevant suttas.

I have also included in this section hypothetical **questions-and-answers** that enable me to explain the Buddha's teaching in greater detail. Examples of such questions are: (1) Could you please explain on what basis the Buddha attained full enlightenment? (2) Could you please explain the four characteristics that the Buddha mentioned at the beginning of the sutta on the Law of Dependent Origination and the Law of Dependently Arisen Phenomena? (3) Could you please explain how the Buddha clearly recognized the cycle of arise-remain-decay-cease-transform that applies to all worldly phenomena? (4) What are unconditioned phenomena and what are conditioned phenomena? (5) Could you please explain the connection between the saying "See your true nature and become Buddha" in Chinese Zen Buddhism and the process by which Buddha attained full enlightenment? (6) What is the law of cause and effect in Buddhism?

I consider the two processes of the Buddha's spiritual cultivation and realization and his full enlightenment as core knowledge in Buddhist meditation. This is the reason why I always teach the Buddha's process of spiritual cultivation, realization and enlightenment at the beginning of the Fundamental Meditation course and the Intermediate Meditation courses. In 1999, I started writing a series of books entitled "Understanding and Practice of Buddhist Meditation", the first of which is "The Buddha's Process of Spiritual Cultivation and Realization". Eight years later, as the need for teaching grew, I re-published the book "The Buddha's Process of Spiritual Cultivation and Realization" together with three new books dedicated to meditation practice. They are: "The Effect of Meditation on People's Life", book 1 and 2, and the last book of the series, "Commentaries on Meditation in Question and Answer Format", published in 2007.

I have applied this approach to all teaching courses that I have conducted in California, Oregon, Texas, Florida, Washington D.C., Virginia as well as in Canada, Australia, Germany, France and Switzerland. I am now collating all these teaching materials into this book, under the title of **"The Buddha's Process of Spiritual Cultivation, Realization and Enlightenment – A Treatise and Commentaries in Question and Answer Format"**.

Examining the four Buddhist holy sites

Between 2000 and 2011, I organized seven pilgrimages to "the Buddha's homeland" for meditation students to explore the four holy sites that relate to the Buddha's life, spiritual practice, realization and enlightenment, and teaching. My aim in conducting these trips was to get a close and clear appreciation of the locations that I mention in "The Buddha's Process of Spiritual Cultivation, Realization and Enlightenment", and to ensure that there is correspondence with objective reality. I have personally

INTRODUCTION

taken pictures at these locations and included them in this book.

Most noteworthy are two groups of pictures (1) at Bodh Gaya and (2) at the Self-Mortification Forest. I spent considerable time studying these two sites. I discovered that Bodh Gaya, which was constructed by King Aśoka based on the recommendations of the fourth Buddhist patriarch Upagupta, commemorates the events following the Buddha's enlightenment at seven sites but makes no reference to the Buddha's four stages of spiritual realization. This means that the Buddha's realization of the Law of Dependent Origination has been placed at the fourth week. However, if we take into consideration the four weeks in which the Buddha attained his spiritual realization, we would say that the realization of the Law of Dependent Origination occurred in the eighth week.

BOOK SUMMARY

GENERAL CONSIDERATIONS

Meaning of Bodhisattva

According to Buddhist traditions, a Bodhisattva (*Bodhisatta* in Pāli) is a spiritual practitioner who has vowed to become enlightened and save him/herself first, then teach the truth that has been realized in order to guide others who believe in his/her teaching to help them attain what s/he has attained. Bodhisattva also has the meaning of someone who aspires to become a Buddha.

In the Pāli suttas, before he became enlightened, the Buddha often called himself Bodhisatta. Following this tradition, in this book, I will call Prince Siddhattha "the Bodhisattva" in the period after he renounced his princely life to go into the forest in search for a spiritual master. He was then a person who followed a spiritual practice with the aim to attain enlightenment and liberation first for himself, and then to help guide others to the other shore. The Buddhist saying for this is "enlighten oneself, enlighten others; attain ultimate enlightenment".

Significance of the self-mortification practice

The practice that led to the Buddha's enlightenment and ultimate liberation was based on the four stages of samādhi and not on self-mortification. However, if he had not spent many long years practicing self-mortification, fighting the cravings and demands of the senses, in particular the mind's habits of *inner talk*[1] and *inner dialogue*[2], he would not have been able to easily vanquish the false mind and progressively internalize the four stages of samādhi, and through these, attain enlightenment as his *Tathā*-mind shone through. For this reason, I speak highly, in this context, of the value of the self-mortification practice of the Bodhisattva.

This point is self-evident. After 29 years living in the midst of luxury, lavishness and sensual pleasures, the Buddha's mind could not easily forget in a short period of time the sensations and passions associated with material pleasures. The long years of self-mortification practice carry a high significance that the meditation student should be aware of. We cannot underestimate the struggle against the desires of the self. If we overlooked the self-mortification practice of the Bodhisattva, we could fail to see the factors on which his spiritual realization was based. We might just see the Bodhisattva leave the practice of yoga meditation, then abandon the practice of self-mortification, then apply the method of "Awareness of Breathing In, Breathing Out" for several weeks, and finally sit in meditation for four weeks to achieve enlightenment. In this view, attaining enlightenment would appear so easy! In reality, things are not that simple.

Vanquish the factors that agitate the mind

The Yoga meditation practice and the harsh self-mortification practice enabled the Bodhisattva to later easily control his mind. The energy of mental defilements could no longer dominate his mind. Consequently, the Bodhisattva was able to easily attain the four samādhi stages by applying the *breathing in, breathing out* technique that he discovered. The most difficult among these stages was samādhi without inner talk and inner dialogue (*avitakka-avicāra samādhi*).

The long years practicing self-mortification carried a high significance in the Bodhisattva's eventual attainment. First, self-mortification was a means to control the false mind and vanquish the energy of desires by the self. The most critical part of this struggle was vanquishing the agitating energy of mental defilements. As a result, the inner conflicts within his mind were calmed. This eventually led to the Bodhisattva's *awareness energy* becoming stable and strong. His "self" lost prominence and mental defilements no longer had the energy to agitate his mind. From this foundation, he could easily progress through the samādhi stages.

The six years of self-mortification practice also demonstrated the Bodhisattva's steely determination to attain self-liberation. Hunger, thirst, the bitter cold during many winters spent without clothing to protect his body; the scorching sun during many hot summers; and the terror of living alone in the deep forest did not discourage him. However, when he saw the destruction that self-mortification caused to his body, he had an immediate awakening and decided to abandon the practice. He chose a new method, the Middle Path, which eschewed severe punishment to, as well as inordinate gratification of the body. The Middle Path is really a method that forgoes the dualistic mind but instead focuses on developing the **awareness** energy of the holy mind in spiritual practice.

Without experiencing the extreme harshness of the self-mortification practice, the Bodhisattva would not have been able to *realize* its reverse significance. That is extreme self-mortification only destroys the body and does not help the practitioner develop his/her spiritual wisdom. But excessive self-indulgence also has detrimental effects on the mind. The mind becomes addicted to the pleasures, and forgets about its vow for self-liberation and helping others.

INTRODUCTION

With his practical mind, the Bodhisattva recognized the value of a healthy body. He saw that the body is the necessary and only vehicle that the mind must use to attain higher wisdom and *Nibbāna*. By contrast, his five companions in the self-mortification practice only recognized the value of the mind while ignoring the body. They despised the Bodhisattva, thinking that he had given in to self-indulgence, and left him.

If we use the terminology of Zen Buddhist Minding the Buffalo metaphor, we can say that the five companions focused only on "minding the buffalo" while forgetting about the "cart". The buffalo might be tamed, but if the cart is broken, the buffalo still would not be able to pull it and "bring the owner home".

This is the reason why I entitle this book *"The Buddha's Process of Spiritual Cultivation, Realization and Enlightenment – A treatise and Commentaries in Question and Answer Format"*.

CHAPTER SUMMARIES

This book consists of four chapters.

Focus of Chapter I

The First Awakening

The Great Question: Growing up in a royal family, Prince Siddhattha saw the three laws that govern the life of all human beings – aging, sickness and death – and identified the cause behind this condition as "being born". This is the cause that needs to be eliminated in order to attain the everlasting **Unborn**. The greatest question that preoccupied Prince Siddhattha was how to escape the four laws of **birth, aging, sickness and death in order to attain the Unborn, higher wisdom and *Nibbāna***. This was what differentiated Prince Siddhattha from an ordinary prince. This great question eventually led to a great solution for the entirety of humanity through specific methods of spiritual practice.

With his determination to achieve his higher aspirations, he decided to leave the palace, sever his emotional ties to his family, forgo the material pleasures, luxury and lavishness of palatial life, and go in search of a way to escape birth, aging, sickness and death. This was his first awakening.

Focus of Chapter II

The second awakening

Search for a solution: After quietly leaving the palace, the Bodhisattva lived a homeless life and went deep into the forest in search of teachers. He met two famous teachers of the time who taught him two advanced meditation methods called "The Base of Nothingness" and "The Base of Neither

Perception nor Non-Perception". In a short period of time, the Bodhisattva attained these two high levels of Yoga meditation. However, he was disappointed when he recognized that these two high levels did not help him meet his objectives of escaping birth, aging, sickness and death, and attaining the Unborn, higher wisdom and *Nibbāna*. He left the teachers, and the methods that did not meet his objectives, to search for other methods that could lead him to his goals.

This was his second awakening. The Bodhisattva recognized that on the spiritual path, **the teaching is more important than the teacher**. The Bodhisattva would not pay respect to a teaching that did not meet his goal of escaping birth, aging, sickness and death, and attaining the Unborn, higher wisdom and *Nibbāna*, even though the teacher might have a large following.

The third awakening

Self-mortification practice: From Rājagaha, the capital of the Kingdom of Magadha, the Bodhisattva wandered through the forest and found his way to the Uruvelā area which had a river, white sandbanks and populated areas that made begging for food in the village possible. He decided to stay there to practice.

While he was still searching for a practice method that met his objectives, he met a group of monks led by Koṇḍañña who was living in the hills near Uruvelā beside the Phalgu River. This group taught the Bodhisattva the self-mortification practice. They proposed that through self-mortification, one would be able to attain higher wisdom and *Nibbāna*. The Bodhisattva was overjoyed and placed his full trust in the guidance of Koṇḍañña.

The Bodhisattva followed the practice of the group, but he adopted the most extreme forms of self-mortification. He used willpower in his strong determination to vanquish the desires of the self.

The result was that the Bodhisattva was able to "crush" all the old habits of desires and passions that he had accumulated since his youth from two sources: from his genes and from the traditions of his family, caste, and religion that he had been learning from birth to the age of 29. However, higher wisdom failed to spring forth, and *Nibbāna* remained elusive, while his body became so emaciated that he could no longer walk. He finally fainted and nearly lost his life. He realized that he had to abandon the self-mortification practice.

This was his third awakening.

Focus of Chapter III

1. Reviewing the self-mortification practice

The Bodhisattva reviewed the self-mortification practice with regard to its effect on his mind and on his body. He remembered the breathing technique that he had used when he was about ten years old.

2. Starting a new journey

He knew that the breathing technique can lead to a deep samādhi state. He decided to abandon the self-mortification practice, and resumed eating normally. When he had recovered his health, he began practicing the breathing method that he had discovered. His five self-mortification companions were upset with him and went elsewhere to continue their practice.

The Bodhisattva entered the decisive stage of his spiritual journey. He started with the breathing method that he had experienced in his youth.

3. Key points of the process of spiritual cultivation and realization

Favorable causal conditions

Once he recovered his health, the Bodhisattva left the self-mortification forest, crossed the Phalgu River, and chose a spot where many large banyan trees grew, to sit in meditation. A young woman named Sujāta, the daughter of a wealthy land owner, made him an offering of nutritious *kheer* cake. With the help of this offering, the Bodhisattva did not need to go begging for food, and could forgo eating for several weeks and practice until he attained enlightenment.

The practice environment

In order to have a quiet place to practice, the Bodhisattva crossed the Nerañjarā River, chose a spot underneath a large *pipphala* tree (also called a *pipal* tree) which had a large crown, and laid down *kusha* grass as a sitting meditation mat.

He then made a solemn vow: *"Even if my skin, sinews, bones as well as my flesh and blood were to become dry, I will not leave this place unless I have attained the supreme enlightenment"*.

The Bodhisattva then meditated for four consecutive weeks without sleep, using his breathing method and passing through four stages of Samādhi, each with unique results.

- **First week**

The Bodhisattva used the *single thought awareness with silent talk* technique to practice **breathing**, silently saying: "I know I am breathing in, I know I am breathing out", "I know I am breathing in a short breath, I know I am breathing out a long breath". He practiced this technique day and night for one week and experienced a state of *samādhi with inner talk and inner dialogue,* and a sense of elation and bliss. This feeling of elation and bliss was generated by his mind being in a state of deep stillness. This samādhi state was later called Preliminary Samādhi or Preliminary Meditation stage.

- **Second week**

The Bodhisattva continued practicing breathing by maintaining a *silent awareness of **his in-breath, and out-breath***, without focusing his mind on anything. After a week, he experienced the state of *samādhi without inner talk and inner dialogue*[3]. In this state, he experienced a greater feeling and sensation[4] of elation and bliss. At this samādhi stage, the language formation process which consists of inner talk and inner dialogue became totally silent, and his mind became unified[5]. This samādhi state is classed as the Second Meditation stage.

- **Third week**

The Bodhisattva continued applying his breathing technique but now used his **awake awareness**. Subsequently he experienced a **full and clear awareness**: *a clear and complete awareness without any attachment to that awareness*. The thought formation process, consisting of the Feelings and Sensations aggregate and the Perception aggregate, became completely still. His mind became

INTRODUCTION 17

completely serene, without any attachment to the feeling of elation and bliss. He called this state "letting go of elation and dwelling in equanimity". This samādhi stage was later classed as Clear Awareness Samādhi (*Sampajañña-Samādhi*), or Third Meditation stage, or Equanimity[6].

- **Fourth week**

The Bodhisattva experienced his breath automatically stopping and restarting at intervals. *The language formation process and the thought formation process were completely silent.* At that time, the Bodhisattva's mind became totally empty and still. All that remained was a continuous flow of *bare cognition* about the surrounding environment that contained no trace of verbal chatter in it. The Bodhisattva described this mental state as "*as such*" or "*tathā*". This state was totally "outside the realm of reasoning" (*atakkāvacara*). The Bodhisattva saw that his mind was totally malleable, pure, unblemished and wieldy... This samādhi stage was later classed as the Fourth Meditation stage or the **Immobility of the Three Mental Formation Processes** stage. The three mental formation processes consist of the language formation process, the thought formation process and the bodily function formation process. They all became immobile.

The empty and still state of mind that the Bodhisattva had entered has been called the "***tathā*-mind**". "*Tathā*" means "as such" or "as thus". This is a mind in an impregnable immobility state. This immobility has been called immobility mass (or samādhi aggregate[7]). In this state, there is only *a bare cognition, a clear and wordless awareness.* From a neuroscience perspective, the samādhi aggregate corresponds to the Wernicke area, whereas the clear and *wordless* cognitive awareness corresponds to the precuneus which is located in the parietal lobe of the rear left and right hemispheres of the brain. Developmental Buddhist Masters often described this state of mind as "a clear mind that reflects all things".

The essence of Buddhist meditation is founded upon this *tathā*-mind state. From this state, the potential for enlightenment, or the Buddha-nature of the Bodhisattva progressively emerges.

The *tathā*-mind is the result of the immobility of the three mental formation processes, where the most important stages are the immobilization of the language formation and thought formation processes. The immobility of the bodily formation process refers to the breath automatically stopping and re-starting. It is a consequence of the immobility of the language formation and thought formation processes.

The immobility of the language formation process occurs when verbal chattering stops arising automatically in the mind. This verbal chattering consists of the *inner talk* and *inner dialogue*. Both become silent. The second samādhi stage corresponds to the *samādhi without inner talk and inner dialogue* stage. The immobility of the thought formation process is the result of the Feelings and Sensations aggregate and the Perception aggregate becoming inactive. This corresponds to the third samādhi stage, also called the *"letting go of elation, dwelling in equanimity"* stage.

Full and complete realization (Abhisamaya)

Following that, through the three watches of the last night, the Bodhisattva attained full and complete realization of the "Three Insights".

INTRODUCTION 19

1. On the first watch of the night, corresponding now to the period from 7pm to 10pm, he saw his past lives, from one past life to thousands of past lives. This is called the "Insight into One's Own Past Lives".

2. On the second watch of the night, corresponding now to the period from 10pm to 1am, he saw the birth and death, gathering and separation of all living beings, the causes of their birth and death and the causes of their happiness, wealth, subservience, misery, hardship, power, social status, caste, occupation; their gender and appearance; disasters and good fortunes that befall them; their happiness, peace of mind, sorrow, suffering, extreme hardship. He saw that the character of all living beings was shaped by the three forms of karma – action karma, speech karma and intention karma – that create a chain of causes and effects. There was no punishment or reward by any divinity. This is called the "Insight into the Divine Vision".

3. On the third watch of the night, corresponding now to the period from 1am to 4am, he saw the Four Noble Truths and saw that mental defilements are the cause for the cycle of birth and death. These mental defilements consist of three categories: desires, craving for existence and ignorance. Once mental defilements are extinguished, the cycle of birth and death is also terminated. This is called the "Insight into the Termination of Mental Defilements".

Finally, the Bodhisattva was cleansed of all defilements. He experienced liberation. Rebirth was terminated. The holy life was accomplished. All that had to be done was done. After this life, he would not be reborn in any of the six realms of the world. He had truly attained the **Unborn**.

Focus of Chapter IV

Realization of the Law of Dependent Origination

The key part of the Buddha's process of enlightenment was his realization of the Law of Dependent Origination and the Law of Dependently Arisen Phenomena. While he dwelt in his *tathā*-mind, he looked upon worldly phenomena and saw that they had four characteristics:

1. Suchness (*Tathatā*).
2. Indivisibility (*Avitathatā*)
3. Identicalness (*Anaññathatā*)
4. Specific conditionality (*Idappaccayatā*)

The Buddha classified the first three characteristics as belonging to unconditioned phenomena, whereas the fourth belonged to conditioned phenomena.

He saw that worldly phenomena evolved according to an order; however this order was not established or organized by a divinity. There is no divinity who determines a certain direction for worldly phenomena to follow. The Buddha was merely someone who realized the nature of worldly phenomena. These evolved according to an orderly sequence that he identified as: Arise, Remain, Decay, Cease and Transform.

Inside each worldly phenomenon resides an energy called "change and transformation". This energy is the cause that drives all changes in worldly phenomena.

Using his enlightened vision, the Buddha saw that the core of all conditioned phenomena is "Emptiness" (Pāli: *Suññatā*). Emptiness is the cause that resides at the heart of the law of change and transformation. Looking at human beings, he searched for the original cause that led to the creation of humans. He identified twelve causal conditions that lead to the creation of humans: (1) Ignorance gives rise to Mental Formations, (2) Mental Formations give rise to Consciousness, (3) Consciousness gives rise to Name and Form, (4) Name and Form gives rise to the Six Senses, (5) the Six Senses give rise to Contact, (6) Contact gives rise to Feelings and Sensations, (7) Feelings and Sensations give rise to Desires, (8) Desires give rise to Possession, (9) Possession gives rise to Craving for Existence, (10) Craving for Existence gives rise to Birth, (11) Birth gives rise to Aging and Death (12).

Death is not the end of the cycle as it leads to rebirth in what is called the "cycle of birth and death". The cycle of birth and death is a continuous process set in motion by what the Buddha called the "force of karma". The Buddha identified karma as the cause that governs the fate of humans. As long as humans continued to live under the influence of karma, the cycle of birth and death would continue endlessly.

Consequently, when looking at the nature of the Self, the Buddha saw that this Self is in reality a cycle of continuous change. When we try to find a primordial Self, we can't find one. On this basis, the Buddha said that the Self in reality does not exist; it is a No-Self. However, inside this Self there is the energy of change and transformation that causes changes in the twelve causal conditions that create a human being. For this reason, one cannot find the original cause that creates humans, nor can one find the cause that terminates their existence.

Emptiness is the cause that creates all things and all phenomena. It is considered the true nature of phenomena.

Conditioned phenomena are phenomena that are created by their specific conditionality (*idappaccayatā*) which contains the energy of "change and transformation". The law of change and transformation governs the whole of the universe and humanity. The Buddha contemplated the Law of Dependent Origination through the three watches of the night and summarized it in these four lines of verses:

Because this is, that is;
Because this arises, that arises;
Because this is not, that is not;
Because this ceases, that ceases.
(Khuddaka Nikāya, Udāna, Ud 1.3)

Suchness (*tathatā*) is considered the essence of the phenomenal world. The Buddha compared it to the **Unborn**. It is not created because it does not depend on anything. It is as vast as the infinite void, but it differs from the void because it does not have the capacity to contain anything.

Through his enlightenment, the Buddha became the historical Buddha, meaning a Buddha that existed in reality. He was 35 years of age.

Notes on Buddhist terms

I would like to say a few words about the matter of explaining the Buddhist terms used in this book.

In writing this book, my focus has been to reach readers who have no prior knowledge of Buddhist meditation, including the younger Vietnamese people who were not born in Vietnam or have left Vietnam more than 40 years ago and now live in America or other countries. This is why I have attempted to use common language to explain the meaning of the more technical terms used in Buddhist and Zen Buddhist texts.

I consider meditation as a science like any other science because its aim is to serve humanity. It does not address material matters such as physics, chemistry, geology, biology, etc., but spiritual matters such as the development of intuitive wisdom and the adjusting and balancing of body and mind that other sciences do not address. This is why I believe that meditation should be explained clearly and systematically. It should not be an activity reserved for those who seek liberation for themselves and confine themselves to isolated, high-walled temples and meditation centers. On the contrary, meditation has always been an integral part of the multi-faceted daily life of all of us. If we know how to exploit its unique methods and apply them to our everyday life, achieving inner peace is really within our reach. Our body and mind will be in harmony and intuitive wisdom will shine in us.

This is the reason why, when unfamiliar Buddhist words occur in the text, I try to use comparable English words to explain their meaning. I hope that readers who wish to befriend meditation can easily grasp the meaning of technical terms used in Buddhist and Zen Buddhist texts, either through words in their native language, or English words comparable to the Chinese-Vietnamese ones.

By understanding the meaning and effect of these technical terms, the reader will be able to avoid any unfortunate mistake when practicing meditation.

To help readers with Buddhist and Zen Buddhist technical terms, I have included an explanation of these terms in the Notes section of the book. In particular I have included their Pāli, Sanskrit and Vietnamese equivalent where appropriate. My intention is to show the origin of each word, whether it comes from the Pāli or Sanskrit literature. Readers knowledgeable in technical terms need not refer to that section.

I sincerely hope that this book will be of assistance to readers who seek to know more about Buddhist meditation, or who wish to experience its transformative benefits in areas such as changing one's character, achieving harmony between body and mind, and experiencing the flowering of the spiritual intuitive wisdom that is innate in all of us.

Thích Thông Triệt
Vesak, Buddhist Year 2558
Riverside, May 2014

CHAPTER I

THE SUPREME BEING

AND HIS MOTIVATIONS

1

IN SEARCH OF THE LIGHT OF THE BUDDHA'S TEACHING ON MEDITATION

Introduction

As students of meditation, we should be aware of the importance of the process by which the Buddha, the founder of Buddhist meditation, conducted his spiritual cultivation and attained his realization. What motivated him to renounce all that he possessed to go into the forest in search of spiritual teachers? Why did he seek to escape the worldly life[1] full of pleasures, luxuries and magnificent opulence that he enjoyed? How did he come to an early realization that worldly sensuous pleasures[2] and lavishness only result in suffering and endless rebirth? Why did he want to escape the things that satisfied his senses? Why did he want to escape that which was born[3] to seek the Unborn[4]? What causal conditions helped him achieve his goals? What was his teaching?

Furthermore, by studying his spiritual cultivation journey we will be able to clearly identify key themes in the various stages of his spiritual practice:

- What key elements of his meditation practice helped him progress deeper and deeper into the higher samādhi states?

- What were the key elements of the method that he used to discover the Unborn, discard the Born, and find the path to enlightenment and ultimate liberation after six long years of arduous practice? How could we

CHAPTER 1: THE SUPREME BEING AND HIS MOTIVATIONS 27

experience each step that he followed? From this we are able to gain a practical understanding of the source of the spiritual teaching that he has transmitted to posterity. We can also understand clearly why his teaching remains relevant, more than 25 centuries later, to those who choose to practice with a strong sense of self-reliance and a clear intellect. They can put their trust in the Buddha's teaching and practice assiduously to experience for themselves a blissfulness[5], sense of harmony, freedom from concern, serenity and detachment, and eventually experience spiritual wisdom, enlightenment and liberation from birth and death.

Depending on our own personal circumstances, we can then choose the most appropriate method to guide our practice because most of the Buddha's teaching was based on the principle of appropriateness to each individual's spiritual faculty[6] and circumstances. Those who have ample time can choose to go on short or longer retreats. Those who are short on time may practice for 30 minutes or 60 minutes each day, etc. Furthermore, we can practice where it is convenient for us, in our work place or in a park; on a farm or in a factory; while we are driving, going to the toilet, eating a meal, getting dressed, washing dishes or doing our laundry. We can introduce meditation into every activity that we do. Because the key to achieving blissfulness and harmony through meditation resides in activating *one of the ultimate senses of our wordless awareness mind*[7] by one of several methods: "silent awareness", "awake awareness", or "knowing through seeing, hearing, touch without thinking".

The effects of Buddhist meditation

In studying the stages of the Buddha's spiritual practice, we will focus on finding the essence of the method that brought him success. Even if we do not have the goal of becoming enlightened as he did, we can still recognize that we have latent in us what is unborn and not subject to death – our ultimate cognition faculty – and we can appreciate the precious teaching[8] that the Buddha has left humanity. With the right causal conditions, we will be able to adopt a practice that is suitable to our needs and cognitive capacity. Because it is only through *practice* that we are able to change our perspective on life, others, ourselves, our mind and our possessions. This will enable us to experience a transformation in our mind and karma that will bring our body and mind in harmony and eliminate ignorance and attachments from our mind.

We dedicate ourselves to practice to be able to see worldly phenomena[9] – people, things, facts, events – *as they are* using our *ultimate seeing* faculty and not our intellect and consciousness, with their embellishment, elaboration and like-dislike emotions. Over time, we will be able to reduce afflictions such as loving the self, clinging to the reality of the self[10], indulging the sensual pleasures of the self[11], and feeling pride in the self[12]. We will then be able to bring our body and mind into balance and transform our karma. From there, the old habit of attachment to things will progressively be eliminated from our mind, and inner peace and equanimity will be present permanently in our daily life. Life is too short. We should work toward bringing meaning to our life and usefulness to ourselves, our family and those around us.

When causal conditions are met for us to go straight home[13] – the home of the Unborn[14] – we may then make the vow to sever all worldly relationships[15] and all worldly knowledge[16] to start a new journey. A journey where we can go inside our mind to fight the demons of false thoughts and ignorance, as the Buddha once did before finally attaining enlightenment.

CONCLUSION

New wine in an old vessel

In the last 2,500 years, the Buddha's life story has been told in many languages by scholars in many countries. In Vietnam, from the 2nd century AD, when Buddhism was first introduced, to the present day, many scholars, senior monks and Zen Masters have written about the life of the Buddha. One might think that this endeavor to retell what has already been documented over the last 20 centuries is unnecessary. However, when we follow the Buddha's meditation methods, we need to understand the stages through which he conducted his spiritual practice and identify the crucial elements:

1. What difficulties did he face in his spiritual journey?

2. What was his first meditation method?

3. Why did he abandon the Yoga meditation method and the self-mortification practice to finally invent his own new method that led him to ultimate enlightenment?

4. What were the steps in his meditation method and how were they conducted? Why did he consider the consciousness, mind faculty and intellect as impediments to meditation?

5. What were the key factors leading to his ultimate enlightenment?

My whole aim in writing this book is to help us identify a practice method that will bring our body and mind into balance, and eliminate sorrow and suffering from our everyday life. Even though the Buddha's life story has been told in many languages around the world, few among us would have had the opportunity to deeply reflect on it and draw the lessons of his exacting spiritual cultivation journey. How many of us have even a cursory knowledge of the very arduous practice that the Buddha went through so that we can draw inspiration from his experience when we encounter unfavorable conditions?

Inquiry into the above questions is the raison d'être for this book.

The vessel might be old, but it contains new wine. You will find that this wine has novel flavors. They will help you recognize the essential elements that led to the Buddha's enlightenment; the importance of the strenuous efforts that he made in the early part of his journey; and the succinct path that he discovered and taught to mankind after he attained enlightenment.

2

THE HISTORICAL BUDDHA

A new era

Sakkamuni (or Sākyamuni in Sanskrit) is a real historical figure in the civilization of mankind, not an imaginary person born out of people's fertile imaginations.

He was a real person. Although he lived in a human body like any of us, he was more fortunate than most, for he was born into a governing royal family and was endowed with all the luxury and pleasures of life as a prince. He differed from most people in that he recognized at a very early age the suffering that resides at the core of the endless cycle of birth, aging, sickness and death. The reality of his suffering differed from the suffering of ordinary people. His dissatisfactions and internal conflicts were also totally unlike ours. He was not afflicted by suffering and despair caused by his family situation or social standing. He did not give in to despair and run away from the world and from his responsibilities as a father, a husband and a son. He wanted to lift all beings out of the sea of sorrow, having seen how helpless people were in the face of aging, sickness and death.

He decided to renounce his social status in the ruling class, all family ties and the lavishness and luxury of his princely life, to go deep into the forest to find a way first to liberate himself, and then to liberate all other beings.

Through a long journey with numerous hardships, missteps and struggles against his inner demons, he finally reached his ultimate goal: enlightenment and experiencing in his own body and mind both the conventional truth[1] and the ultimate truth[2]. He saw clearly and completely the origin of suffering and the path to cease suffering. He saw *as they are* mental defilements and how to eradicate them. He did not uncover the truth through subjective reasoning and did not learn it from any spiritual teachers. Nor did he seek guidance from any divinity.

It was in his deepest state of despair that he identified through his self-generated wisdom his own novel practice. Then after many complicated practice stages, he finally abandoned all effort and striving to step onto the path toward enlightenment and ultimate liberation.

This is an important point that we need to note.

After attaining enlightenment, and upon the request of Brahmā deity Sahampati, the Buddha decided to teach what he had realized to all those whose ears are willing to hear, whose eyes are willing to see, and especially those who are determined to seek liberation and abandon old beliefs to apply his self-realization approach. The Buddha's teaching was unique in that it was realized[3] through his body, mind and spirituality.

The Buddha's teaching opened a new era – the Era of Enlightenment – based on the creative energy of his own potential for enlightenment. Developmental Buddhism later called this potential for enlightenment our Buddha-nature (*Buddhatā*).

The Buddha's real name

When he was a prince, the Buddha's name was Siddhattha (in Pāli) and his family name was Gotama (in Pāli) or Siddhārtha Gautama (in Sanskrit). After enlightenment, he

CHAPTER 1: THE SUPREME BEING AND HIS MOTIVATIONS

was called Gotama Buddha. His disciples called him "Blessed One" (*Bhagavat*) or "Buddha". People from other religions called him "Friend Gotama" (*Bho Gotama*) or "Monk Gotama" (*Samana Gotama*). When he travelled to teach, people called him Sakkamuni (Sākyamuni in Sanskrit), meaning the silent sage of the Sakka clan. He called himself *Tathāgata* meaning "who has thus come" or "who has attained the ultimate truth through Suchness or the *tathā*-mind".

The Buddha is known in history as the Fully Enlightened One[4] and the founder of Buddhism. Buddhism is also called the "Enlightenment Path" (*Bodhīti magga*) and is one of the world's great religions, philosophies and spiritual sciences. Buddhism as a spiritual science has contributed greatly, through the arts, architecture, literature and philosophy, to the civilizations of India, Sri Lanka, Thailand, Myanmar, Cambodia, Laos, China, Japan, Korea, Mongolia, Tibet and Vietnam as well as Western countries through the Tipiṭaka (the "Three Baskets") consisting of the Sutta (Buddha's discourses) Piṭaka, the Vinaya (rules) Piṭaka, and the Abhidhamma (commentaries) Piṭaka written in Pāli[5] and in Sanskrit[6].

The Pāli texts are used as references by Theravāda Buddhism (or the Southern School[7]) whereas the Sanskrit texts are used as references by the Northern School[8] (or Developmental Buddhism[9]).

In the Dīgha Nikāya ("The Long Discourses of the Buddha") – Mahāpadāna Sutta DN14 ("The Sublime Story"), the Buddha said that there were six Buddhas before him: Vipassī, Sikhī, Vessabhū, Kakusandha, Konāgamana and Kassapa.

Meaning of the word "Buddha"

Buddha is not the name of a person but a designation given to someone who has attained full enlightenment or has personally experienced the ultimate reality that is Suchness or *Tathatā*. This is the first fundamental quality of a Buddha.

According to the Early Buddhist texts, during his enlightenment, the Buddha acquired the "Three Insights"; then through samādhi he acquired other supermundane powers[10] such as the Sixfold Higher Knowledge, the Tenfold Knowledge-Powers, the Fourfold Fearlessness, the Five Eyes, and Omniscience.

When the term Buddha is mentioned in Buddhism, it applies to Sakkamuni, the founder of Buddhism. As such it means "the Enlightened One[11]" or the "Awakened One[12]".

The attribute "enlightened" means that the Buddha attained the highest form of transcendental wisdom[13], which is Suchness wisdom. He had omniscience, was the Fearless One (*Akutobhaya*) and the Teacher of Non-duality (*Advayavādin*). He intimately knew the origin and true nature of worldly phenomena and the causes of sorrow, suffering and the endless cycle of birth and death as they apply to human beings, as well as the way to terminate these. This is because he had attained complete self realization[14] in his body and mind concerning the termination of mental defilements and the cycle of birth and death, and had discovered the path to ultimate liberation.

Through the transcendental power of his Buddha Eye, he knew the character, spiritual capacity, tendencies and thoughts of all beings. He used his omniscience to deliver his teaching so that everyone who listened to him could clearly understand what he taught. This is the second attribute of a Buddha, the ability to enlighten each one according to their level of spiritual development.

As his dual capacity of enlightening-oneself and enlightening-others had reached complete perfection, he was called the Buddha.

He was called "the awakened one" because he had awoken from the deep delusion caused by worldly pleasures. He was no longer misled by ephemeral mirages caused by the veil of ignorance. He was liberated from addiction to worldly pleasures; he had awoken from confusion created by worldly mirages, which had for so many lives ensnared him in a sea of misconception and attachment to illusory pleasures.

He was truly awakened. His wisdom shone bright. Mental defilements[15], clinging to falsehoods, and desires[16] no longer drove his mind toward a passion for the objects of the senses, which generates karma. He clearly saw that all worldly phenomena have the characteristics of impermanence[17], suffering[18] and no-self[19]. He was fully in control of his feelings and sensations for they remained totally still when objects came into contact with his senses. He did not need to subjugate his six senses, and yet his six senses did not get attached to external objects. His unborn wisdom, or his **ultimate cognition faculty**, had become a stable energy that radiated around him and was permanently present in all his activities. It was present during his waking hours and during his sleep, when he walked in meditation and when he delivered his sermons. He saw all phenomena as they are[20], without being distorted or embellished by worldly emotions[21] or clinging to falsehood[22]. He also possessed the skillful means[23] to teach people from all walks of life according to their character and temperament[24] and help them become awakened like he was. After he left this temporary life, he would not be reborn in any of the realms of the world. Due to the two fundamental attributes of enlightening-oneself and enlightening-others, he was called the Blessed One (*Bhagavat*).

3

THE SUPREME BEING

His origins

The future historical Buddha was born a prince belonging to the Khattiya warrior caste who constituted the ruling and military class of the time and to the Sakka (also in Pāli: Sākiyā, Sakyā; Sākya in Sanskrit) clan. His family name was Gotama (Gautama in Sanskrit); he was the eldest son of King Suddhodana and Queen Māyā. His father reigned over the small kingdom of Kosala, with its capital Kapilāvatthu, a fertile area near the Himālaya Mountains in Northeastern India bordering the south of Nepal.

His birth

He was born in Lumbīnī, in the republic of Koliyā, now part of Nepal. According to the traditions prevalent at the time in this area, when a woman was about to give birth, she returned to her family's home in order to be close to her parents and relatives. When Queen Māyā was near giving birth, King Suddhodana organized a delegation to take her from Kapilāvatthu to her home country in Devadaha in the small kingdom of Koliyā. When the group passed through the Sāla forest at Lumbīnī, near the village of Paderia, the Queen gave birth to the Prince. That was the full moon of the fifth month (the Vesākha month, equivalent to the 16th of April to the 15th of May in the current calendar) of year 624 BCE[*]. The Queen's party took her and the Prince back

---

[*] There are many differing theories about the year of birth of the Buddha. Some books have him living in 623-543 BCE; 566-486 BCE; 563-483 BCE; 560-480 BCE; 448-368 BCE; 480-400 BCE. However,

to Kapilāvatthu immediately after the delivery of the Prince as she was in very poor health. Today, this location is in the village of Rummindei, at the border between India and Nepal.

In 1886, Sir Alexander Cunningham (1841-1893), a British Major General of the Royal Engineers and archaeologist, discovered a stone column erected by King Aśoka (273-236 BCE) which commemorated the Buddha's birth place.

(In 1958, King Mahendra of Nepal made a donation to restore the Lumbīnī site which has now become an international Buddhist pilgrimage site. There are currently many temples belonging to both the Southern School and the Northern School of Buddhism around the site.)

---

all agree that he lived to the age of 80. I have chosen 624-544 BCE to match the Buddhist calendar currently in use around the world.

Signs of a great being

One day, the sage Asita who was a hermit living in the Himalaya mountains, King Suddhodana's esteemed teacher and a renowned seer, came to Kapilāvatthu to visit the King and see the newborn prince. When he held the baby in his arms and quietly gazed at him, he noticed that the baby had 32 special marks[1] that were indicative of a great person (*mahāpurisa-lakkhaṇa*). He made a prediction: "If the Prince remains in the palace, he will become a world emperor[2] and the whole world will pay him homage. If he renounces his princely life and becomes a monk he will become a great enlightened being (a Buddha) who will bring salvation to a great number of beings".

Asita was overcome with joy but then cried as he realized that he would not live long enough to witness the baby becoming a great enlightened being and to become his disciple. King Suddhodana was surprised and feared that there were some ill omens regarding the Prince. Asita explained why he laughed and cried. Both he and the King paid respect to the newborn.

Five days later, the King organized the naming ceremony for his son. 108 Brahmin priests were invited, among whom were eight who were specialized in foretelling the future. Seven of them predicted that one of two things could happen to the newborn:

1. When he becomes an adult, if he never witnesses human suffering, he will become a wise ruler of a large kingdom; or

2. If he witnesses human suffering, he will renounce his family to follow the spiritual path and will become a great enlightened being.

Koṇḍañña, the youngest of the eight Brahmin foretellers, was the only one who was adamant that the newborn would become a great enlightened being.

Queen Mahā Pajāpatī Gotamī and Prince Siddhattha

These predictions filled the King with worry. He decided that he would isolate his son from the outside world until adulthood to prevent him from witnessing any human suffering such as aging, sickness and death.

The newborn was named Siddhattha (in Pāli; or Siddhārtha in Sanskrit), meaning "the one who accomplishes his goal." Seven days after giving birth, Queen Māyā passed away, and the second wife of King Suddhodana, Mahā Pajāpatī Gotamī became the one who raised the newborn.

When the Prince came to the age of learning, the King invited Asita and other Brahmin teachers to become his teachers.

Early causal conditions leading to his becoming the historical Buddha

From childhood, Prince Siddhattha showed a preference for silence and solitude. One day, as was the tradition of the Sakka clan, the King together with his court and the population, gathered for the Ceremonial Plowing of the Land[3] festivities to celebrate before starting the agricultural season. While everyone was enjoying the celebrations, Prince Siddhattha sat cross-legged under a rose-apple (*jambu*) tree with his back straight and started **breathing in and out while maintaining a wordless awareness** of his breath, oblivious to the noise and activities around him.

His servants had all gone away to enjoy the celebrations. When they came back, they saw the Prince sitting in the lotus position with a tranquil and silent mind apparent on his serene and innocent face. They were so surprised to see the young Prince sitting peacefully in meditation that they ran to the center of the ceremony to report to the King what they saw.

(This was the early experience which later helped the Prince open a new horizon in his practice and led him to attain enlightenment and ultimate liberation.)

The King hurriedly went to the rose-apple tree and saw the Prince still sitting there, peaceful and silent like an experienced yogi (*yogin*). He silently clasped his hands to pay respect to the Prince a second time. He admired his son for being able to keep a still mind like an experienced yogi; at the same time, what he saw concerned him.

He remembered the sage Asita's predictions and saw that this was a sign that the Prince had causal conditions of spiritual practice from past lives. How could a ten-year old boy be able to keep a still mind in meditation like experienced Yoga practitioners? The thought preoccupied him, and he felt more concern than joy.

He worried that the destiny of the Prince would not accord with his own plans. He was concerned that when the Prince reached adulthood, he would leave him, the palace and the throne to search for the truth and spiritual masters, as Asita and the Brahmin priests had predicted. If this came to be, who would succeed him to rule over this fertile land?

Back at the palace, the King started thinking about a plan to isolate the Prince and prevent him from entering into contact with the outside world. He invited all renowned teachers to come and teach the Prince all matters, from cultural subjects, the arts to martial arts. He also created an environment for the Prince to enjoy all the pleasures and luxury of palatial life. He was determined to get the Prince addicted to these pleasures so that he would abandon any thought of leaving this world for a spiritual life.

The temptation plan

When the Prince reached adulthood and started to appreciate the pleasures of the senses, King Suddhodana built for him three palaces for his enjoyment: a *Ramma* palace for winter, a *Suramma* palace for summer, and a *Subha* palace for the rainy season. Each palace had hundreds of young, beautiful, elegantly dressed, lavishly ornamented and jeweled women skilled in singing and dancing. They attended him day and night. Their role was to satisfy the senses of the Prince, ensnare him in materialistic pleasures and draw him away from any thoughts of leaving his family.

The King gave the following orders to those responsible for running the inner city:

- The Prince must not see any sad events inside the inner city.

- The Prince must not be allowed to see old, sick or dead people or cremation ceremonies.

- The Prince must only see young, beautiful and healthy people, and joyful and vibrant scenes.

The King thought that, if the Prince was surrounded in this way, he would only see pleasurable and joyful events and would not be moved by sad ones. This would prevent him from thinking about leaving the family and following a spiritual path.

Reality turned out to be different. Although the Prince experienced all these pleasures, he did not become addicted to them. Once the causal conditions were met, he had the resolve to leave everything behind.

Later on, the Buddha recounted to his disciples his life of luxury and pleasures in these terms:

Bhikkhus, I was delicately nurtured, most delicately nurtured, extremely delicately nurtured. At my father's residence lotus ponds were made just for my enjoyment: in one of them blue lotuses bloomed, in another red lotuses, and in a third white lotuses. I used no sandalwood[4] unless it came from Kāsi[5] and my headdress, jacket, under garment[6], and robe[7] were made from cloth from Kāsi. By day and night a white canopy was held over me so that cold and heat, dust, grass, and dew would not settle on me.

I had three mansions: one for the winter, one for the summer, and one for the rainy season. I spent four months of the rains in the rainy-season mansion, being entertained by musicians, none of whom were male, and I did not leave the mansion. While in other people's homes slaves, workers, and servants are given broken rice together with sour gruel for their meals, in my father's residence they were given choice hill rice, meat, and boiled rice. (Aṅguttara Nikāya ("The Numerical Discourses of the Buddha") – Book of the Threes 3.39 ("Delicate")

Marriage to bind the Prince to worldly life

In order to permanently bind the Prince and eliminate his thoughts of leaving the princely life and becoming an ascetic recluse, the King planned to have him married. He thought that if the Prince found a beautiful, virtuous, intelligent and clever wife, she would keep him forever bound to palatial life. For this wife would deeply love him and bear him beautiful and bright children. The Prince would feel duty-bound to care for his wife and children. He would also feel the need to be more virtuous and more talented than others in order to ensure a happy life for his wife and children. The King would encourage him to excel at the cultural arts and the martial arts. In this way, he hoped that he would fulfill Asita's predictions that the Prince might become a world emperor instead of a great enlightened being.

As soon as the Prince turned 16, the King put his plan into action and married him to Princess Yasodharā, one of his first cousins, also aged 16.

Thirteen years later, when the Prince was 29, he had become a handsome young man, intelligent, strong and skilled in martial arts. King Suddhodana thought that he had succeeded. He thought that the Prince would never find the opportunity to follow the spiritual path, but would become his worthy successor.

Causal conditions arrive

When the Prince turned 29, he asked his father for permission to see how the people lived outside the palace walls.

The King agreed to the Prince's request but he also arranged for the Prince to witness only the happy and prosperous life of the population outside the palace. He ordered that all houses along the Prince's path must be elegantly and brightly decorated to greet the Prince. The Prince's charioteer, Channa, was instructed to lead the Prince through the pre-arranged path.

At the age of 29, the Prince was ready to determine the sources of suffering of human beings through the three stages of aging, sickness and death that he witnessed when he travelled outside the palace. He saw that if he continued to live engrossed in luxury and pleasures, he would one day fall into aging, sickness and death as he had witnessed during his trips. He saw that aging, sickness and death are laws from which no human beings could escape, and he thought about the meaninglessness of human life: one was born, grew up, enjoyed the pleasures of the world, and then fell into aging, sickness and death. With his strong will, he did not want to give in to this fate. He wanted to forgo all luxury and pleasures and retreat into the forest to find a way to escape aging, sickness and death. Even though at the time he had a young son by Yasodharā, he was still determined to leave the palace, live a homeless life, and withdraw from the world to practice like the monk that he had seen on his fourth trip outside the palace. He considered this to be the best way forward.

The stories about the life of the Buddha mention that it was not until he was 29 years old that he knew about aging, sickness, death and spiritual practice, based on what he saw on his trips outside the palace.

CHAPTER 1: THE SUPREME BEING AND HIS MOTIVATIONS   47

First encounter: an old person

When he was just outside the palace, the Prince saw among the joyful crowd a person with a bent back walking with the help of a stick and looking miserable. The Prince was surprised because he had never seen inside the palace such a weary and miserable person trudging along. He asked Channa why this person had a bent back, a pale complexion and wrinkled skin, and why he looked weary and haggard and trudged along unlike the other happy people around.

Channa explained that this person with wrinkled skin and a pale complexion used to be a young man with physical strength and a healthy complexion like everyone else. However, as the years accumulated, he lost his strength and some of his teeth, he could not eat as well as in his youth; his skin started to wrinkle and become pale and his hair turned white. Eventually, he became an old person, with hollow cheeks, poor eyesight and a bent back, and needing to lean on a stick to walk. This person is called an old person.

The Prince was surprised and asked Channa why this person was called an old person. Channa answered that it was because he did not have long to live. The Prince thought about himself and asked Channa whether he too would one day become an old person.

Channa told the Prince that every person in this world would become old, weak, with missing teeth, white hair, poor eyesight, wrinkled skin, hollow cheeks and bent back. No one could avoid the fate of becoming old and weak. Anybody who had been born would become old and weak. One day, the Prince would also become old like this old person.

On hearing Channa's explanations, the Prince concluded that aging is a law that governs all human beings. One day, he too would become old, weak and miserable like this old person. His physical strength, health, alertness and vivacity would disappear.

The Prince started to become preoccupied by the fate of aging that no person in this world could avoid. He saw that humans are powerless against aging. He no longer wanted to continue his excursion and ordered Channa to turn back toward the palace.

Second encounter: a sick person

Another day, the Prince and his charioteer Channa went outside the palace again. This time he saw a very sick person who suddenly fell and urinated uncontrollably. Full of surprise, he asked Channa why this person suddenly fell and urinated uncontrollably, why his eyes didn't look like those of other people, and why the sound of his voice was also unlike that of other people.

Channa explained to him that this person was sick and that any person might experience sickness.

The Prince asked Channa whether he too would one day fall sick. Channa responded that one day the Prince would become sick like the person he had seen.

The Prince was further puzzled. Why could no person ever avoid falling into sickness? A feeling of sadness arose within him as he realized that sickness is a law that applies to all human beings. No one could avoid sickness because the human body is always subject to sickness. Everyone will one day get sick. He no longer wanted to continue his

CHAPTER 1: THE SUPREME BEING AND HIS MOTIVATIONS 49

excursion and ordered Channa to turn back toward the palace.

Third encounter: a dead person

Another time, as they were going further from the palace, the Prince witnessed a procession of people with sad eyes who were carrying a person lying immobile and covered with a white cloth. The Prince asked Channa: why was that person lying immobile? Why were the other people sad and crying? Where were they carrying the immobile person?

Channa explained that the person who was lying immobile and covered with a white cloth was a dead person and the other people were taking his body to be cremated. They were people close to the dead person. They were sad and crying because they knew they would never see the dead person again.

The Prince asked Channa whether some day he would be dead also. And whether the King and the Queen and any of his close ones would see him again afterwards, and whether he would be able to see them.

Channa responded that death is the last day of a person's life, and a dead person would never see anyone again. What was left of a person after death was only a dead body!

The Prince was deeply shocked by what he heard and started thinking that one day he would be dead and would not be able to see anyone again. Full of sorrow, he ordered Channa to immediately turn back toward the palace.

On his way back, the Prince realized that death is a law that applies to all human beings. No human being could avoid it.

For several days, the Prince could not recover his peace of mind. The scenes of aging, sickness and death kept reappearing in his mind. He realized that human beings are totally powerless when faced with death. Wealth, happiness, luxury, lavishness, material pleasures, and power would eventually end up as an immobile body taken to the funeral pyre.

What he saw made a powerful impression on his mind. He did not know who he could consult to discuss solutions to end aging, sickness and death. One day, he also would become aged, sick and dead. And he would leave everything behind and not be able to see anyone again.

The Prince realized how meaningless a human life is. Being born, growing up, enjoying material pleasures, and then falling into sickness, aging and eventually death! Death is a law from which no one can escape.

With indomitable determination, he refused to succumb to this law. From time immemorial, human beings had been powerless when faced with the laws of aging, sickness and death. He must find a way to free himself from these three harsh laws so that he could help all other people to do likewise.

Meanwhile, Princess Yasodharā was about to give birth. The Prince could feel that the burden of family responsibilities would soon weigh on him. A deep gnawing sadness arose in his mind.

Fourth encounter: a monk

One early morning, to ease his heavy mind, the Prince rode alone outside of the palace on his horse Kanthaka. He eased the reins to let Kanthaka run far from the capital

Kapilāvatthu. He soon arrived in peaceful countryside and settled down to rest under a tree. From a distance he saw a person with a shaved head and dressed in a yellow robe walking toward him at a leisurely pace.

The person's steps were relaxed, yet full of dignity and quiet peace. He was draped in a yellow robe and had his head and face shaved. The Prince was filled with surprise because he had never seen this type of person inside the palace.

When the person came near, the Prince saw someone with a serene and pure face, a radiant complexion and a shaved head and face carrying a bowl in his two hands. He asked the questions that puzzled him: How did you achieve this peaceful, serene and silent state of mind? What is your occupation? Why do you wrap yourself in a yellow robe? Why do you shave your head and face? Why are you wandering alone? Where is your home?

The person calmly answered the Prince's questions. The Prince learnt that he was a monk who lived a homeless life; that his spiritual practice kept his mind serene; that as a monk he should shave his head and face, wrap himself in a robe, leave his family, live a homeless life, sleep under a tree or in a cave, beg for food, and practice in order to attain the highest goal of escaping aging, sickness and death. He was currently pursuing the bliss that comes with liberation from birth, aging, sickness and death.

On hearing these words, the Prince felt as though he had awakened from a dream. He realized that this was the answer to the questions that had preoccupied him in the last few days. He immediately thought about how he could live a homeless life, leave his family, shave his head and face, wrap himself in a yellow robe, beg for food and pursue self-liberation like this monk.

Happiness began to appear on the Prince's determined face. He bid farewell to the monk and got back on his horse to return to the palace with lightness and excitement in his heart. He had found a new direction to his life: he would leave his family, shave his head and face, wrap himself in a yellow cloth, live a homeless life, beg for food and pursue the bliss of self-liberation from birth, aging, sickness and death.

REFERENCES

FOR CHAPTER I

1. Encyclopedia of Buddhism, Government of Sri Lanka, 1971, Editor: G.P. Malasasekera, O.B.E. Book 1, pp. 97-98; Book 3, pp. 207-208, 224-225, 249-251, 357-371, 490-495, 572-574; Book 4, pp. 478-480.

2. The Life of Buddha, by A. Ferdinand Herold, Tokyo, Japan 1954, pp. 12-67, 81, 85-86.

3. Banner of the Arahants, by Bhikkhu Khantipalo, Sri Lanka, 1997, pp. 1-4.

4. The Gospel of Buddha, by Paul Carus, London, 1995, pp. 8-25.

5. The Buddha and His Dhamma, by Dr. B.R. Ambedkar, Taiwan, 1997, pp. 5-9; 32-39; 45.

6. Dimensions of Buddhist Thought, by Francis Story, Sri Lanka, 1976, pp. 3-8; 14-20.

7. Buddhist Scriptures, by Edward Conze, England, 1959, pp. 35-52.

8. Buddhism, by Kenneth K.S. Chen, Woodbury, New York, 1968, pp. 18-19.

9. The Buddha, by Sukumar Dutt, M.A., PH.D., New Delhi, 1955, pp. 18; 26-27; 31.

10. Indian Buddhism, A Survey with Bibliographical Notes, by Hajime Nakamurā, New Delhi, 1987, pp. 18-19.

11. Buddhism in Translations, by Henry Clarke Warren, New Delhi, 1986, pp. 48-49.

12. Dictionary of Pāli Proper Names, New Delhi, 1998.

13. The Numerical Discourses of the Buddha, A Translation of the Aṅguttara Nikāya, by Bhikkhu Bodhi, Boston, 2012, AN 3:39.

CHAPTER II

THE INVALUABLE EXPERIENCE

1

THE FIRST JOURNEY:

LEAVING HOME TO SEEK

THE SPIRITUAL PATH

The awakening of the Supreme Being

When he returned to the palace, the Prince felt energized by the image of the wandering, begging monk who vowed to practice spirituality in order to find liberation. He knew what the path that he should take looked like.

Looking at his life, he realized that this life full of luxury, lavishness and pleasures was the seed of birth, aging, sickness and death. This was something that he had not realized in the long period up to that moment. Luxury and pleasure had always filled his mind. He never lacked for songs, music, abundant alcohol and meat, the fragrance of beautiful women and sensual pleasures. His senses and feelings were always caught in the vortex of passions and pleasures. He realized that *as someone who was himself subject to birth, he was seeking whatever was subject to birth; as someone who was himself subject to aging, sickness, death, suffering and defilement, he was seeking whatever was subject to aging, sickness, death, suffering and defilement.* Wife, children, possessions, gold, silver, a high status in life, servants, domestic animals, etc. were all subject to birth, aging, sickness, death, suffering and defilement. He now clearly realized that as long as his mind remained entrapped in a life dedicated to luxury and pleasure, and to satisfying the desires of the senses with things that were subject to birth, aging, sickness, death, suffering and defilement, he would not be able to escape birth, aging, sickness and death. He realized that family life is a life tainted by the dust of worldly concerns. If he left his family to live in the vastness of the outside world, uncluttered by sorrow, his mind would be more pliable to purification.

This was the first realization of the Supreme Being.

The unshackling

From then on, the Prince saw as a necessary condition for escaping birth, aging, sickness and death a determined abandonment of all that was born to seek the Unborn. This consisted of freeing himself from his family to live a homeless life, severing the bonds of worldly love and renouncing the high status that he had. If he remained in the palace, his mind would be forever caught in worldly matters. Leaving home was a necessary condition for his quest to find a spiritual method, and then learning and practicing it with the aim of terminating birth, aging, sickness and death. If he stayed with his family, he would never be able to attain these lofty goals.

Indeed, only a Supreme Being could come up with such a momentous awakening.

The Majjhima Nikāya ("The Middle Length Discourses of the Buddha") recounts his state of mind at the time:

Household life is crowded and dusty; life gone forth is wide open. It is not easy, living in a home, to practice the holy life[1] utterly perfect and pure as a polished shell. Suppose I shave off my hair, put on the yellow robe, and go forth from the home life into homelessness? (Majjhima Nikāya, "The

Middle Length Discourses of the Buddha", Mahāsaccaka Sutta #36, "The Greater Discourse to Saccaka", MN 36:12)

The Noble Search

The Majjhima Nikāya, "The Middle Length Discourses of the Buddha", Ariyapariyesanā Sutta, "The Noble Search", Sutta #26 describes thus the Prince's frame of mind:

Bhikkhus, there are these two kinds of search: the noble search and the ignoble search. And what is the ignoble search? Here someone being himself subject to birth seeks what is also subject to birth; being himself subject to aging, he seeks what is also subject to aging; being himself subject to sickness, he seeks what is also subject to sickness; being himself subject to death, he seeks what is also subject to death; being himself subject to sorrow, he seeks what is also subject to sorrow; being subject to defilement, he seeks also what is subject to defilement. (MN 26:5)

The Buddha enumerated what is subject to birth: *Wife and children, men and women servants, goats and sheep, fowl and pigs, elephants, cattle, horses and mares, gold and silver are subject to birth.*

The Buddha talked about the significance of him, being born, seeking what is subject to birth: *These objects of attachment are subject to birth; and one who is tied to these things, infatuated with them, and utterly committed to them, being himself subject to birth, seeks what is also subject to birth.*

He also described his awakening:

Bhikkhus, before my enlightenment, while I was still an unenlightened Bodhisattva, I too, being myself subject to birth, sought what is also subject to birth; being myself subject to aging, sickness, death, sorrow, and defilement, I sought what is also subject to aging, sickness, death, sorrow, and defilement. Then I considered thus: 'Why, being myself subject to birth, do I seek what is also subject to birth? Why, being myself subject to aging, sickness, death, sorrow, and defilement, do I seek what is also subject to aging, sickness, death, sorrow, and defilement? Suppose that, being myself subject to birth, having understood the danger in what is subject to birth, I seek the unborn supreme security from bondage, Nibbāna. (MN 26:13)

From that time, he made the decision to leave his family and seek the Unborn in what he considered a noble search. He could no longer live the worldly life, even though he was advised that Princess Yasodharā had just given birth to his first son. That was a crucial determination by the Supreme Being to pursue the spiritual path. This determination would be a deciding factor in the attainments of the future Buddha.

The dawn of enlightenment started to appear

Right in the middle of the night, before leaving and possibly never seeing Princess Yasodharā again, the Prince walked softly into his wife's bedroom, and stood there to take a final look at his wife and his newborn son to honor his relationship with his wife. He then silently walked quickly out of the room.

This was a crucial decision by the Supreme Being. This was the dawn of the enlightenment path for humanity.

Outside, Channa had already prepared his horse and waited for him. When the Bodhisattva came out, Channa silently handed over the reins to him. The Bodhisattva silently jumped onto his horse, with Channa riding behind him.

When he was outside the city's gates, the Bodhisattva pressed his feet onto Kanthaka's sides. The horse neighed loudly, breaking the silence of the night, and broke into a fast gallop. He ran swiftly in the direction desired by the Bodhisattva.

Leaving Kapilāvatthu, they took the Uttarāpatha road (the Northern Road) and arrived in the morning at the Anomā River in Magadha country. Kanthaka had covered a distance of 30 yojanas, or about 120 km.

There the Bodhisattva removed his jewelry, cut his beautiful hair and gave it all to Channa. He also exchanged his princely clothes with Channa's ordinary ones (some books indicate that he exchanged his clothes with a hunter). Finally, he told Channa to return to the palace and inform King Suddhodana that he was determined to leave his family and seek liberation. He would return to Kapilāvatthu to meet the King and his stepmother Queen Pajāpatī once he had conquered aging and death, experienced the end of the Born and attained the Unborn.

The emotions of animals

Channa accepted his mission and sadly rode Kanthaka back to the palace. Kanthaka was also sad. He knew that he would never see his beloved master again. Not long after, Kanthaka had a tremor in his chest, burst his heart and died.

2

SEARCHING FOR SPIRITUAL TEACHERS

According to the Pāli suttas, during the period that he was searching for teachers of the spiritual path, the Buddha called himself Bodhisattva which meant a person who had abandoned the worldly life, severed all bonds of worldly love, and was determined to seek enlightenment and liberation for oneself first, and then to guide other living beings to the other shore.

A marvelous causal condition

From the Anomā River, the Bodhisattva reached the Anupiya mango grove. He temporarily stayed there for seven days. From Anupiya, he walked into Rājagaha to beg for food.

Rājagaha was the capital of Magadha and was about 30 yojanas from the Aromā River. In those days, Magadha was one of the four largest kingdoms in India. King Bimbisāra reigned over this kingdom. He ascended to the throne when he was just 15 years old. When the Bodhisattva left his family, King Bimbisāra had reigned for nine years. He was 24 years old, while the Bodhisattva was 29.

One day, as was his custom, the Bodhisattva entered Rājagaha to beg for food. King Bimbisāra was standing on an upper story when he observed through a window a young monk carrying a begging bowl and walking lightly in a calm and deliberate way. The King was very surprised by what he saw and asked his guard to follow the monk, learn where he was staying and inform the King when he had

CHAPTER 2: THE INVALUABLE EXPERIENCE

completed his begging round and had eaten so that the King could come and pay him a visit in person.

His guard did as he was instructed. Once he had informed the King that the monk had finished eating, the King mounted his horse and rode to the place indicated by the guard.

King Bimbisāra exchanged salutations with the Bodhisattva and learned that he was the son of King Suddhodana of Kapilāvatthu. King Bimbisāra noticed the calm and dignified demeanor of the Bodhisattva, his logical reasoning, clear elocution, and his lofty goals and aspirations. The King was full of admiration and invited the Bodhisattva to join him and govern the large kingdom of Magadha. The Bodhisattva clasped his hands and politely declined, saying that his objective when he left his family was to terminate the Born and search for the Unborn, for enlightenment and liberation. Upon hearing this, the King respected the Bodhisattva even more and knew that this monk was not someone of ordinary caliber.

King Bimbisāra knew that he could not sway the Bodhisattva's resolve and politely wished the Bodhisattva to attain the fruit of enlightenment soon. He also asked that, in the first year after the Bodhisattva had attained enlightenment, he would come to Rājagaha to teach the King and his people. The Bodhisattva silently acquiesced.

The King was filled with joy and mounted his horse to return to his palace, hoping that he would see the Bodhisattva again in Rājagaha after he attained enlightenment.

Second awakening: the teaching is more important than the teacher

Traveling through the forest, the Bodhisattva encountered many outstanding teachers, in particular Āḷāra Kālāma in Vaiśālī and Uddaka Rāmaputta in Rājagaha, the capital of Magadha. Both teachers were very famous, had many disciples and taught meditation according to the Yoga tradition, specializing in samādhi meditation. The teaching that the Bodhisattva received from both teachers was excellent, however these two methods of samādhi meditation did not help him achieve his goal of terminating birth, aging, sickness and death. In the end, he had to bid farewell to both teachers to search for other methods. He realized that the teaching is more important than the teacher. If the teaching could not take him to where he wished to go, he had to leave the teacher, even though the teacher had many disciples. This was the second awakening of the Bodhisattva.

The first teacher

Āḷāra Kālāma taught the Bodhisattva a meditation method called the Base of Nothingness[2], which was the third level of the Formless Meditation (*Arūpa Jhāna*) method. After a short period of time, by exercising a maximum level of effort, the Bodhisattva reached this level of meditation and reported his success to his teacher. Āḷāra Kālāma was delighted but admitted that he had nothing else to teach him. He could only ask the Bodhisattva to stay and teach new disciples. The Bodhisattva turned down the offer as his purpose was to seek the bliss of liberation and not to teach others while his mind was not yet peaceful and pure, his higher wisdom was yet to shine bright, and he was yet to experience enlightenment and *Nibbāna*.

The second teacher

The Bodhisattva reluctantly bid farewell to his first teacher and continued his quest for the right teaching. His second teacher was Uddaka Rāmaputta who taught him the Neither-Perception-nor-Non-Perception[3] method.

After a short period of time, by exercising a maximum level of effort, the Bodhisattva successfully reached the state of Neither-Perception-nor-Non-Perception. This was the highest level in Yoga meditation[4]. The teacher was delighted and again invited the Bodhisattva to stay and teach others.

But the Bodhisattva considered that this was not his ultimate goal as it did not meet the aspirations that he had when he left his family and renounced his life of luxury and lavishness. He wanted to eradicate mental defilements, sever the tangled web of thoughts, eliminate all concepts and thinking, avoid all that was born, terminate greed and desires, develop his spiritual wisdom, attain enlightenment and be liberated from all worldly realms, which is *Nibbāna*. By contrast, the state of Neither-Perception-nor-Non-Perception was still mired in the realm of *the Born* as the mind was still caught in delusions; the tangled web of thoughts was still not severed and enlightenment was yet to be experienced.

So, for the second time, the Bodhisattva had to reluctantly leave his teacher because the method taught by the teacher did not help him achieve the goal that he had when he left the palace.

He wandered in the forest around Magadha determined to find a teaching that would help him attain the Unborn, the sublime peace, the higher wisdom, and *Nibbāna*. Or, in other words, a method that would lead to the termination of birth, aging, sickness and death.

Assessment of the samādhi meditation methods of the two teachers

To bring more richness in this text, I include here the Buddha's own assessment of his first two teachers after he had attained enlightenment. (Majjhima Nikāya, "The Middle Length Discourses of the Buddha", Ariyapariyesanā Sutta #26, "The Noble Search", MN 26:14 to MN 26:16).

First he described his motivations when leaving his home, then assessed his first teacher. He said:

Later, while still young, a black-haired young man endowed with the blessing of youth, in the prime of life, though my mother and father wished otherwise and wept with tearful faces, I shaved off my hair and beard, put on the yellow robe, and went forth from the home life into homelessness.

Having gone forth, Bhikkhus, in search of what is wholesome, seeking the supreme state of sublime peace[5], I went to Āḷāra Kālāma and said to him: 'Friend Kālāma, I want to lead the holy life in this Dhamma and Discipline'[6]. Āḷāra Kālāma replied: 'The venerable one may stay here. This Dhamma is such that a wise person[7] can soon enter and abide[8] in it, realizing for himself through direct knowledge his own teacher's doctrine.'

Through strenuous practice, the Bodhisattva attained in a short period of time the Base-of-Nothingness state – the third stage of Yoga meditation. In this state, the practitioner senses the state of "nothingness" surrounding him/her while sitting in meditation and after the sitting meditation session. In this process, while the mind is not agitated nor attracted to objects, it still perceives "nothingness" surrounding with a silent and permanent flow of "nothingness" thoughts. The Base-of-Nothingness is a type of samādhi created by the I-Consciousness[9]. It results in stillness of the intellect, but does not entirely stop the silent verbal chattering in the mind. It is still a manifestation of *the Born*; the consciousness is no longer affected by the external world but is still present. For these reasons, the Bodhisattva recognized that this method did not help him achieve a peaceful and pure mind, the end of desires, and liberation. He said:

I soon quickly learned that Dhamma. As far as mere lip-reciting and rehearsal of his teaching went, I could speak with knowledge and assurance, and I claimed, 'I know and see' – and there were others who did likewise...

Then I went to Āḷāra Kālāma and asked him: 'Friend Āḷāra Kālāma, is it in this way that you declare that you enter and abide in this Dhamma by realizing for yourself with direct knowledge?' – 'That is the way, friend.' – 'It is in this way, friend, that I also enter upon and abide in this Dhamma by realizing for myself with direct knowledge.'

Upon hearing the Bodhisattva, Āḷāra Kālāma was delighted and invited him to stay and guide other students. The Bodhisattva declined. He saw that the Base-of-Nothingness method did not help him eliminate delusions, forsake greed and desires, achieve a peaceful and pure mind, higher wisdom, enlightenment, and *Nibbāna*, but only resulted in a state of "nothingness". He left and sought other teachers.

The Buddha recounted the praise of Āḷāra Kālāma:

– 'It is a gain for us, friend, it is a great gain for us that we have such a venerable one for our companion in the holy

life. So the Dhamma that I declare I enter upon and abide in by realizing for myself with direct knowledge is the Dhamma that you enter upon and abide in by realizing for yourself with direct knowledge... So you know the Dhamma that I know and I know the Dhamma that you know. As I am, so are you; as you are, so am I.'

He also recounted the invitation from Āḷāra Kālāma:

'Come, friend, let us now lead this community together.'

The Buddha further recounted his thoughts at the time:

Thus Āḷāra Kālāma, my teacher, placed me, his pupil, on an equal footing with himself and awarded me the highest honor. But it occurred to me: 'This Dhamma does not lead to disenchantment[10], to dispassion[11], to cessation[12], to peace[13], to higher wisdom[14], to enlightenment, to Nibbāna, but only to reappearance in the base of nothingness.' Not being satisfied with that Dhamma, I left and went away.

The Bodhisattva then went to practice under his second teacher, who taught him the Neither-Perception-nor-Non-Perception method. He said:

Still in search, Bhikkhus, of what is wholesome, seeking the supreme state of sublime peace, I went to Uddaka Rāmaputta and said to him: 'Friend Uddaka, I want to lead the holy life in this Dhamma and Discipline.' Uddaka Rāmaputta replied: 'This Dhamma is such that a wise man can soon enter upon and abide in it, himself realizing through direct knowledge his own teacher's doctrine.'

The Bodhisattva was then instructed in the Neither-Perception-nor-Non-Perception method. This method was not based on faith but on self-knowledge, clear self-

CHAPTER 2: THE INVALUABLE EXPERIENCE 69

awareness, self-accomplishment, and then abiding in this method. He described his thoughts thus:

I considered: 'It was not through mere faith alone that Rāma declared: 'By realizing for myself with direct knowledge, I enter upon and abide in this Dhamma.' Certainly Rāma abided knowing and seeing this Dhamma.' Then I went to Uddaka Rāmaputta and asked him: 'Friend, in what way did Rāma declare that by realizing for himself with direct knowledge he entered upon and abided in this Dhamma?' In reply Uddaka Rāmaputta declared the base of neither perception nor non-perception.

Through strenuous practice, the Bodhisattva achieved a short time later the state of Neither-Perception-nor-Non-Perception. He recounted:

I considered: 'Rāma is not the only one to have faith, energy, mindfulness, concentration, and wisdom. I too have faith, energy, mindfulness, concentration, and wisdom. Suppose I endeavor to realize the Dhamma that Rāma declared he entered upon and abided in by realizing for himself with direct knowledge.'

Following that, he went to Uddaka Rāmaputta and reported to him the results of his practice. He said:

I soon quickly entered and abided in that Dhamma by realizing for myself with direct knowledge. Then I went to Uddaka Rāmaputta and asked him: 'Friend, was it in this way that Rāma declared that he entered upon and abided in this Dhamma by realizing for himself with direct knowledge?'

Rāmaputta replied: – *'That is the way, friend.'*

The Bodhisattva said: – *'It is in this way, friend, that I also enter upon and abide in this Dhamma by realizing for myself with direct knowledge.'*

Upon hearing the Bodhisattva, Rāmaputta invited him to stay and teach others with him:

– *'It is a gain for us, friend, it is a great gain for us that we have such a venerable one for our companion in the holy life. So the Dhamma that Rāma declared he entered upon and abided in by realizing for himself with direct knowledge is the Dhamma that you enter upon and abide in by realizing for yourself with direct knowledge... So you know the Dhamma that Rāma knew and Rāma knew the Dhamma that you know. As Rāma was, so are you; as you are, so was Rāma. Come, friend, let us now lead this community together.'*

The Bodhisattva declined the invitation. He considered that the Neither-Perception-nor-Non-Perception method did not lead to his goal of attaining enlightenment and liberation. If he stayed and taught others, he would become a teacher like Rāmaputta. This would be a waste of effort. Once again, he left and went away. He recounted:

Thus Uddaka Rāmaputta, my companion in the holy life, placed me in the position of teacher and accorded me the highest honor. But it occurred to me: 'This Dhamma does not lead to disenchantment, to dispassion, to cessation, to peace, to direct knowledge, to enlightenment, to Nibbāna, but only to reappearance in the base of neither perception nor non-perception'. Not being satisfied with that Dhamma, I left it and went away. (Majjhima Nikāya, "The Middle-Length Discourses of the Buddha, Ariyapariyesanā Sutta #26, "The Noble Search", MN 26:14 to MN 26:16)

REFERENCES

FOR CHAPTER II

Sections 1 and 2

SUTTAS

1. Kinh Trung Bộ (Majjhima Nikāya) – Translated into Vietnamese by Hòa Thượng Thích Minh Châu, Saigon, 1986, pp. 364-373 and p. 527

2. The Middle Length Discourses of the Buddha – A New Translation of the Majjhima Nikāya – Translated by Bhikkhu Ñāṇamoli and Bhikkhu Bodhi, Wisdom Publications, Boston, 1995, MN 36:12, MN 26:5, MN 26:13 to MN 26:16

COMMENTARIES

3. The Life of Buddha, by A. Ferdinand Herold, Tokyo, Japan, 1954, pp. 60-70.

4. Banner of the Arahants, by Bhikkhu Khantipalo, Sri Lanka, 1997, p. 1.

5. The Gospel of Buddha, by Paul Carus, London, 1995, pp. 25; 29-31.

6. The Buddha and His Dhamma, by Dr. B.R. Ambedkar, Taiwan, 1997, pp. 35-40; 63-65.

7. The Buddha and His Teachings, by Mahāthera Nārada, Sri Lanka, 1964, pp. 4-5.

8. History of Theravāda Buddhism in South-East Asia, by Kanai Lal Hazra, New Delhi, 1996, p. 12.

3

THE SECOND JOURNEY:

SELF-MORTIFICATION

A new method: Self-Mortification

Although he did not find a way to reach enlightenment and liberation with the Yoga meditation method, the Bodhisattva did not give in to discouragement, and continued his search for a method and a teacher with whom he could practice.

One day, he arrived in a forest in the Uruvelā (now Bodh Gayā) area within the kingdom of Magadha. He saw that this location had high hills, and rivers where one could bathe; it was surrounded by villages where one could go begging for food. He deemed this place very suitable for someone who was determined to practice to attain liberation and decided to choose it for his spiritual retreat. He still did not know what method he would use to practice.

Every day, he went into the villages to beg for food.

A short time later, he met a group of five monks (*Pañcavaggiyas*) whose leader was Koṇḍañña, the other four being Mahānāma, Bhaddiya, Vappa and Assaji. The Bodhisattva knew them since they were previously at the court of King Suddhodana. They taught him the self-mortification[1] practice.

Self-mortification practice

Self-mortification (*duṣkara-caryā; tapas*) was a spiritual practice method that rejected all pleasures and basic comfort for the body; severely restricted desires over long periods; focused on leading an ascetic life without basic comfort, using techniques such as forcing the body, fasting, and punishing the body through several practices applicable to living, sleeping, eating, and clothing. There were seven types of self-mortification practices:

1. Restricting eating to a strict minimum, such as eating one grain of sesame, or one grain of rice or drinking one drop of fruit juice a day.

2. Sleeping on beds of thorns.

3. Living completely naked.

4. Living near a cemetery or deep in the forest.

5. Living like animals such as dogs, cattle, snakes, or chickens.

6. Spreading mud, ash, or powdered charcoal over the body and face.

7. Leaving one's hair and beard uncut and wearing filthy clothes.

Objectives of self-mortification

Self-mortification is a spiritual practice that is traditional to several religions in India. It requires the practitioner to exert strong willpower to vanquish the mind and all demands from the senses. It is in reality a method to oppress the mind – using the worldly mind to vanquish the worldly mind.

According to ancient religious traditions prevalent in India, self-mortification practitioners believed that this method could help them avoid rebirth in the human realm, going instead to a heavenly realm after death. The practice would also provide superpowers and exceptional insights, making the practitioner worthy of being called a holy man. The Bodhisattva believed the explanations of the five monks. He thought that this was a good opportunity for him to experience the superpowers and exceptional insights worthy of a holy man.

The Bodhisattva and the five monks in the Koṇḍañña group practicing self-mortification

Total belief in the self-mortification method

Although he practiced with the five monks, the Bodhisattva chose special practices that were much more brutal. At times, he lived separated from the group as he practiced solitary living, living alone in the wild forest facing his fears. He learned several valuable lessons during this period.

With regard to self-mortification by fasting, no one in the Koṇḍañña group could rival him. He progressively reduced his food intake; from fasting for several days, he finally reached the point where he would eat only a single grain of rice and drink a few drops of fruit juice in a day.

Results of self-mortification

According to the Majjhima Nikāya ("The Middle Length Discourses of the Buddha") Part One, the Bodhisattva's self-mortification practice resulted in a body that was just skin and bones, with hair and beard all falling out. Finally, he was so exhausted that he fainted and fell face down. He was rescued by a passing young shepherdess who fed him some sheep milk, thus he regained consciousness.

He recognized that the self-mortification method did not help him attain enlightenment and liberation, but he also saw that physical pain could no longer influence his mind. His mind became stable. Passions and addictions to the desires of the senses could no longer influence his mind, nor could they urge him to meet their demands. He had vanquished his desires. His mind was no longer attached to, and dependent on, the five desires, craving and sloth. He considered that he had vanquished the armies of his internal demons.

This was a special experience that had the effect of helping the Bodhisattva eradicate the habits of greed and desires of the self. He had eliminated all desire defilements – one of the four categories of mental defilements – that continuously agitate the mind and give rise to cravings. They are normally very difficult to vanquish.

The utmost self-mortification

In the Mahāsīhanāda Sutta, "The Greater Discourse on the Lion's Roar", sutta #12 of the Majjhima Nikāya ("The Middle Length Discourses of the Buddha"), MN12:44 to MN 12:64, the Buddha recounted to Venerable Sāriputta the four ways to torture the body that he practiced over several years. He considered that he was unequalled in four areas:

1. In regard to self-mortification, oppressing the body, self-torturing the body, fasting over several years, he considered that he was unequalled. There was nobody in the world that could fast more than he did.

2. In regard to living in filthy conditions, there was nobody in the world that could be filthier than he was. He had been the filthiest person.

3. In regard to being careful to not cause harm in the tiniest detail, he was the most careful person.

4. In regard to living in isolation, having no contact with any human being over several years, he was the person who had lived most secluded.

The third awakening

The practices enumerated above show that the Bodhisattva's determination to attain liberation was the greatest. Nobody in the world could emulate him. He did so because he believed that such forms of utmost self-mortification would help him achieve his goal of escaping birth, aging, sickness and death, attaining higher wisdom and being worthy of being called a holy man. However the results did not live up to his expectations. They only helped him vanquish his passions and desires, but did not help him develop spiritual wisdom and attain enlightenment and liberation, meanwhile damaging his body. He became exhausted, lost all his physical strength, could not walk or sit steadily and fell down unconscious. At that time, he realized that the self-mortification method was not the right method. This was his third awakening. He decided to abandon the tradition of extreme self-mortification.

Forms of self-mortification

The Buddha recounted the forms of self-mortification that he practiced:

- Living naked.

- Using his tongue to lick his hands clean instead of using water.

- Standing in one place when begging for food instead of going from house to house; anyone who wished to donate food needed to go to where he stood to make their offering.

- Furthermore, he would choose what food he would accept; he would refuse alcohol, meat and fish.

He said:

Such was my asceticism, Sāriputta, that I went naked, rejecting conventions, licking my hands, not coming when asked, not stopping when asked; I did not accept food brought or food specially made or an invitation to a meal; I received nothing from a pot, from a bowl, across a threshold, ...; I accepted no fish or meat, I drank no liquor, wine or fermented brew.

Furthermore, he restricted his eating, such as eating only once a fortnight and eating indiscriminately wheat grass, millet seeds, scraps from hide, rice husk, grass, fruits and roots. He said:

I took food once a day, once every two days... once every seven days, and so on up to once every fortnight; I dwelt pursuing the practice of taking food at stated intervals. I was an eater of greens or millet or wild rice or hide-parings or moss or ricebran or rice-scum or sesamum flour or grass or cowdung. I lived on forest roots and fruits, I fed on fallen fruits.

With regard to clothing, he collected discarded pieces of cloth used to wrap dead bodies, washed them and put them together. Over the years, he used several materials to cover his body such as the bark of the *tititaka* tree, the hide of black mountain goats, or cloth made by weaving hair or horsetail.

He said:

I clothed myself in hemp, in hemp-mixed cloth, in shrouds, in refuse rags, in tree bark, in antelope hide, in strips of antelope hide, in kusa-grass fabric, in bark fabric, in fabric from wood-shavings, in head-hair, in horsetail, in owls' wings.

Adopting other customs

In addition to the self-mortification practices, he also adopted other customs such as:

- Pulling out his hair and beard.
- Not sitting in the lotus position, only standing or squatting.

CHAPTER 2: THE INVALUABLE EXPERIENCE

- When lying, only lying on thorns or on the ground; lying anywhere and usually lying on the right side of the body.

By using these methods of torturing the body, he thought that the body's demands for pleasure would be eliminated, and his mind would become more pure and stable. The mind would no longer crave food, rest, pleasure, luxury and other comforts. He said:

I was one who pulled out hair and beard, pursuing the practice of pulling out hair and beard. I was one who stood continuously, rejecting seats. I was one who squatted continuously, devoted to maintaining the squatting position. I was one who used a mattress of spikes; I made a mattress of spikes my bed; I made wood planks my bed; I made the bare ground my bed; I often slept on a side; I let dust and dirt cover my body; I dwelt and slept out in the open; I dwelt pursuing the practice of lying anywhere I found a place; I ate putrefied food; I did not drink water; I dwelt pursuing the practice of not drinking water; I bathed three times a night; I dwelt pursuing the practice of bathing in water three times daily including the evening. Thus in such a variety of ways I dwelt pursuing the practice of tormenting and mortifying the body. Such was my asceticism.

Practicing filthy living

- Not washing for several years.

In regard to the practice of living in filthy and decrepit conditions, and letting dust accumulate in masses on his body, he said:

Such was my coarseness, Sāriputta, that just as the bole of a tindukā tree, accumulating over the years, cakes and flakes off, so too, dust and dirt, accumulating over the years, caked off my body and flaked off. It never occurred to me: 'Oh, let me rub this dust and dirt off with my hand, or let another rub this dust and dirt off with his hand' — it never occurred to me thus. Such was my coarseness.

In regard to the practice of living very carefully to ensure that no insects on the ground could be harmed, he said:

Such was my scrupulousness, Sāriputta, that I was always mindful in stepping forwards and stepping backwards. I was full of pity even for [the beings in] a drop of water thus: 'Let me not hurt the tiny creatures in the crevices of the ground.' Such was my scrupulousness.

Practicing living in isolation

To practice living in isolation from human beings, severing all human relationships, isolating oneself, not talking to anybody, the Bodhisattva avoided human contact at all times. This was the period when he lived apart from the Koṇḍañña group, focusing on living in isolation in the thick and terrifying forest and in caves in the Mahākāḷa mountains.

When he saw a cowherd, a shepherd, or a person who went into the forest to gather sticks or grasses, or a forest worker, he would run into hiding.

He later recounted:

Such was my seclusion, Sāriputta, that I would plunge into some forest and dwell there. And when I saw a cowherd or a shepherd or someone gathering grass or sticks, or a woodsman, I would flee from grove to grove, from thicket to thicket, from hollow to hollow, from hillock to hillock. Why was that? So that they should not see me or I see them. Just as a forest-bred deer, on seeing human beings, flees from

Caves in the Mahākāḷa mountains, where the Bodhisattva lived several years in isolation about 2,500 years ago.

grove to grove, from thicket to thicket, from hollow to hollow, from hillock to hillock, so too, when I saw a cowherd or a shepherd... Such was my seclusion.

He also recounted his practice of eating things so filthy that nobody could imitate him, such as eating calf dung or drinking calf urine.

This part was mentioned in the Mahāsīhanāda Sutta, "The Greater Discourse on the Lion's Roar", sutta #12 of the Majjhima Nikāya ("The Middle Length Discourses of the Buddha"), MN 12:49.

Mortifying the body

The Bodhisattva recounted other practices to mortify the body such as:

- Living completely naked in the terrifying forest.
- Basking under a scorching sun in the hot summer months.
- Sleeping outside on cold nights under the falling snow in the winter months without a cloth over his body.

In particular, during this period, his spiritual insights started to emerge.

He said:

I would plunge into some awe-inspiring grove and dwell there — a grove so awe-inspiring that normally it would make a man's hair stand up if he were not free from lust. When those cold wintry nights came during the 'eight-day interval of frost', I would dwell by night in the open and by day in the grove. In the last month of the hot season I would dwell by day in the open and by night in the grove. And there came to me spontaneously this stanza never heard before:

*Chilled by night and scorched by day,
Alone in awe-inspiring groves,
Naked, no fire to sit beside,
The sage yet pursues his quest.*

Practicing equanimity

The Buddha further recounted how he practiced equanimity. He was sleeping in a cemetery, leaning on a skeleton when some cowherd boys came next to him, spat on him, urinated on him, put dirt on his body and used sticks to poke into his ears. No evil thoughts arose in him and he did not say a rough word to them. He kept his mind detached from their malicious and impolite deeds. This was his practice of equanimity. He said:

I would make my bed in a charnel ground with the bones of the dead for a pillow. And cowherd boys came up and spat on me, urinated on me, threw dirt at me, and poked sticks into my ears. Yet I do not recall that I ever aroused an evil mind [of hate] against them. Such was my abiding in equanimity.

Practicing eating less and less

Also in the Mahāsīhanāda Sutta, "The Greater Discourse on the Lion's Roar", the Buddha recounted how he progressively reduced this food intake. From eating a small kola fruit a day, he reduced to eating a sesame seed a day to finally eating one grain of rice a day.

He said:

Through feeding on a single kola-fruit a day, my body reached a state of extreme emaciation. Because of eating so little my limbs became like the jointed segments of vine stems or bamboo stems.

Statue of the Bodhisattva in the caves in the Mahākāḷa mountains: just skin over his skeleton

In another section, he said:

Through feeding on a single grain of rice a day, my body reached a state of extreme emaciation...my limbs became like the jointed segments of vine stems or bamboo stems...my backside became like a camel's hoof...the projections on my spine stood forth like corded beads...my ribs jutted out as gaunt as the crazy rafters of an old roofless barn...the gleam of my eyes sank far down in their sockets, looking like a gleam of water that has sunk far down in a deep well...my scalp shriveled and withered as a green bitter gourd shrivels and withers in the wind and

CHAPTER 2: THE INVALUABLE EXPERIENCE 85

sun...my belly skin adhered to my backbone; thus if I touched my belly skin I encountered my backbone, and if I touched my backbone I encountered my belly skin...if I defecated or urinated I fell with my face on the ground...if I tried to ease my body by rubbing my limbs with my hands, the hair, rotted at its roots, fell from my body as I rubbed.

Yet, Sāriputta, by such conduct, by such practice, by such performance of austerities, I did not attain any superhuman states², any distinction in knowledge and vision³ worthy of the noble ones. Why was that? Because I did not attain that noble wisdom⁴ which when attained is noble and emancipating and leads the one who practices in accordance with it to the complete destruction of suffering. (Mahāsīhanāda Sutta, "The Greater Discourse on the Lion's Roar", sutta #12, Majjhima Nikāya ("The Middle Length Discourses of the Buddha"), MN 12:53 to MN 12:56)

Valuable experiences from the self-mortification practice

In the Mahāsaccaka Sutta, "The Greater Discourse to Saccaka", sutta #36 of the Majjhima Nikāya ("The Middle Length Discourses of the Buddha"), the Buddha recounted his experiences with self-mortification. He told Aggivessana, a philosopher of the Niganthaputta Saccaka school, about the practice methods that he followed before he attained enlightenment. Although these methods did not benefit his body and the development of his spiritual wisdom, they did help his mind vanquish totally the desires and demands of the senses and acquire a strong determination to vanquish the demands of the flesh. His body might be in pain but these sensations of pain did not affect his mind.

He recounted these practices in the following terms.

Practicing repressing the mind

First, he applied this method:

- Clenching his teeth while pressing his tongue to the roof of the mouth cavity, with the aim of crushing all unwholesome thoughts, desires and demands for pleasures that presently assailed him. In this way, he fought these unwholesome thoughts with determination.

He said:

Then, Aggivessana, I thought: 'Suppose, with my teeth clenched and my tongue pressed against the roof of my mouth, I beat down, constrain, and crush mind with mind.' So, with my teeth clenched and my tongue pressed against the roof of my mouth, I beat down, constrained, and crushed mind with mind. While I did so, sweat ran from my armpits.

He compared this method with a strong man seizing the head or shoulders of a weak man to overcome him. Likewise, he applied maximal vigor and effort to vanquish his false mind. But the result was not what he expected. Although the mind stayed still, the body did not experience tranquility but was excited. He realized that his failure was due to excessive effort. He said:

Then, Aggivessana, just as a strong man might seize a weaker man by the head or shoulders and beat him down, constrain him and crush him, so too, with my teeth clenched and my tongue pressed against the roof of my mouth, I beat down, constrained, and crushed mind with mind, and sweat ran down my armpits. And although tireless exertion[5], vigor[6], energy was aroused in me, and unmuddled mindfulness established, my body was aroused and

CHAPTER 2: THE INVALUABLE EXPERIENCE

untranquil[7] because of the painful exertion against the painful feeling. But the painful feeling that arose in this way did not invade my mind or remain.

Practicing breathingless meditation

He then moved on to another method: practicing the breathingless meditation[8].

He applied this method five times. In none of these occasions did he experience a development of spiritual wisdom; on the contrary his body became painful, excited and agitated. However, he drew two lessons from the practice. First, as he exerted excessive effort in the strong hope that through the breathingless meditation method he would attain enlightenment; and second, through his determination and combativeness in enduring the pain to his body; his mind became stable and was not influenced by the pain in the body.

Experiences

Below are his experiences with practicing the breathingless meditation method the first time. He described in these terms:

Then, Aggivessana, I thought: 'Suppose I practice the breathingless meditation.' So I stopped the in-breaths and out-breaths through my mouth and nose. As I did so, there was a loud sound of winds coming out from my earholes. Just as there is a loud sound when a smith's bellows are blown, so too, while I stopped the in-breaths and out-breaths through my mouth and nose, there was a loud sound of winds coming out of my earholes. But although tireless energy was aroused in me and unremitting mindfulness was established, my body was overwrought and untranquil because I was exhausted by the painful striving. But such painful feeling that arose in me did not invade my mind and remain.

The terrifying forest in present-day conditions.

The second time, the breathingless meditation resulted in an acute pain in his head. He described in these terms:

Then, Aggivessana, I thought: 'Suppose I practice further the breathingless meditation'. So I stopped the in-breaths and out-breaths through my mouth, nose, and ears. While I did so, violent winds cut through my head. Just as if a strong man were splitting my head open with a sharp sword, so too, while I stopped the in-breaths and out-breaths through my mouth, nose, and ears, violent winds cut through my head. But although tireless energy was aroused in me and unremitting mindfulness was established, my body was overwrought and untranquil because I was exhausted by the painful striving. But such painful feeling that arose in me did not invade my mind and remain.

The third time, breathingless meditation caused him a pain in the head like one caused by a strong man tightening a leather band around his head. He described in these terms:

Then, Aggivessana, I thought: 'Suppose I practice further the breathingless meditation'. So I stopped the in-breaths and out-breaths through my mouth, nose, and ears. While I did so, there were violent pains in my head. Just as if a strong man were tightening a tough leather strap around my head as a headband, so too, while I stopped the in-breaths and out-breaths through my mouth, nose, and ears, there were violent pains in my head. But although tireless energy was aroused in me and unremitting mindfulness was established, my body was overwrought and untranquil because I was exhausted by the painful striving. But such painful feeling that arose in me did not invade my mind and remain.

The fourth time, a terrible pain arose. He felt as if his belly was cut in half. He described in these terms:

Then, Aggivessana, I thought: 'Suppose I practice further the breathingless meditation'. So I stopped the in-breaths and out-breaths through my mouth, nose, and ears. While I did so, violent winds carved up my belly. Just as a skilled butcher or his apprentice were to carve up an ox's belly with a sharp butcher's knife, so too, while I stopped the in-breaths and out-breaths through my mouth, nose, and ears, violent winds carved up my belly. But although tireless energy was aroused in me and unremitting mindfulness was established, my body was overwrought and untranquil because I was exhausted by the painful striving. But such painful feeling that arose in me did not invade my mind and remain.

The fifth time, he felt as if a terrifying heat arose in his body. He described in these terms:

Then, Aggivessana, I thought: 'Suppose I practice further the breathingless meditation'. So I stopped the in-breaths and out-breaths through my mouth, nose, and ears. While I did so, there was a violent burning in my body. Just as if two strong men were to seize a weaker man by both arms and roast him over a pit of hot coals, so too, while I stopped the in-breaths and out-breaths through my mouth, nose, and ears, there was a violent burning in my body. But although tireless energy was aroused in me and unremitting mindfulness was established, my body was overwrought and untranquil because I was exhausted by the painful striving. But such painful feeling that arose in me did not invade my mind and remain.

By then, his body was as exhausted as the body of a dead person. However, although his body was exhausted, his mind remained clear and awake. At that moment, he perceived the thought-waves of the deities – heavenly beings that lived in the area. They were commenting on him. He said:

Now when the deities saw me, some said: 'The recluse Gotama is dead.' Other deities said: 'The recluse Gotama is not dead, he is dying.' And other deities said: 'The recluse Gotama is not dead or dying; he is an Arahat, for such is the way Arahats abide.'

CHAPTER 2: THE INVALUABLE EXPERIENCE

Experience with talking with deities

As he saw that the breathingless meditation method was not effective, he thought about changing into the self-starvation method. But his plan did not come to fruition because the deities caught his thoughts and advised him to abandon it. If he had not accepted their advice, they would have found their own ways to keep his body healthy. Because only with a healthy body could the mind have the means to continue the spiritual practice.

He said:

Then, Aggivessana, I thought: 'Suppose I practice entirely cutting off food'. Then deities came to me and said: 'Good sir, do not practice cutting off food. If you do so, we shall infuse heavenly food into the pores of your skin and you will live on that'. I considered: 'If I claim to be completely fasting while these deities infuse heavenly food into the pores of my skin and I live on that, then I shall be lying.' So I dismissed those deities, saying: 'There is no need.'

Reducing food intake to a minimum

Not being able to self-starve, he decided to reduce his food intake to a minimum. He would sip only a few drops of broth from legumes a day. His body became very emaciated, making his entire skeleton visible.

He said:

Then, Aggivessana, I thought: 'Suppose I take very little food, a handful each time, whether of bean soup or lentil soup or vetch soup or pea soup.' So I took very little food, a handful each time, whether of bean soup or lentil soup or vetch soup or pea soup. While I did so, my body reached a state of extreme emaciation. Because of eating so little my limbs became like the jointed segments of vine stems or bamboo stems. Because of eating so little my backside became like a camel's hoof. Because of eating so little the projections on my spine stood forth like corded beads. Because of eating so little my ribs jutted out as gaunt as the crazy rafters of an old roofless barn.

At that time, the complexion of his skin lost its bright color and became dark.

Now, Aggivessana, when people saw me, some said: 'The recluse Gotama is black.' Other people said: 'The recluse Gotama is not black, he is brown.' Other people said: 'The recluse Gotama is neither black nor brown, he is golden-skinned.' So much had the clear, bright color of my skin deteriorated through eating so little.

Reassessing the self-mortification practice

In the six years that the Bodhisattva practiced self-mortification, he endured terrible pain beyond what any recluse or Brahmin had experienced in the past and in the future. He still did not attain a superhuman state, nor the exceptional vision and insights worthy of a holy man. He started to have doubts about this practice of mortifying the body in countless terrible ways. Eventually, he decided that extreme self-mortification does not lead to enlightenment. He surmised that there would be another path to enlightenment, but he did not know what this path was. At that point, he started to re-assess the extreme self-mortification practice. He concluded that, although this practice did not lead to ultimate enlightenment, his mind had gained tangible results through the strenuous effort:

- It had become entirely cleansed and stable, undisturbed by present painful bodily sensations; avoiding self-praise and being critical of others; not craving and being caught in worldly matters; no longer demanding worldly pleasures; not feeling arrogance, self-importance and pride in the self.

- Past feelings could no longer find their way to arise in his mind.

- Demons (*māra*) inside his mind such as the desire demon (*kāma*), the discontentment demon (*arati*), the hunger and thirst demon (*khuppipāsā*), the craving demon (*taṇhā*), the sloth and torpor demon (*thīna-middha*), the fear demon (*bhaya*), the doubt demon (*vicikicchā*), etc. could no longer arise in his mind to trouble him.

- He assiduously practiced samādhi meditation.

These were positive results that helped his mind reach a stable and tranquil state that he had not experienced previously. He considered himself a warrior who had vanquished the "army of demons".

However, these accomplishments were not the ultimate goal that he wished to attain. He was still not able to attain what he intended and wanted to attain, which was a superhuman state, exceptional vision and insights, worthy of a holy man.

Doubt

The Buddha recounted his state of confusion, agitation and doubt to Aggivessana:

Then, Aggivessana, I thought: 'Whatever recluses and Brahmins in the past have experienced as painful, racking, piercing feelings due to their exertion, this is the utmost, there is none beyond this. And whatever recluses and

Brahmins in the future will experience as painful, racking, piercing feelings due to their exertion, this is the utmost, there is none beyond that. And whatever recluses and Brahmins at present experience as painful, racking, piercing feelings due to their exertion, this is the utmost, there is none beyond this. But by this racking practice of austerities I have not attained any superhuman states, any distinction in knowledge or vision worthy of the holy ones[9]. Could there be another path to enlightenment?'

Remembering an old experience

Once the Bodhisattva recognized that self-mortification, despite its benefits in eliminating internal demons and vanquishing the demands of the body, did not lead to enlightenment and liberation but only to the enfeeblement of the body, he was determined to find a new spiritual practice. He considered that self-mortification had run its course and to continue it would be wrong.

He then remembered the experience of meditating under the rose-apple (*jambu*) tree during the Ceremonial Plowing of the Land festivities organized by King Suddhodana when he was ten years old.

As he was just a child, he did not participate in the traditional festivities. He was also left alone under the rose-apple tree as his servants had run away to enjoy themselves. He ignored the activities around him, sat in the lotus position under the shade of the tree, held his back straight, and focused his mind on his regular breathing. A while later, although he still heard clearly all the noises around him, his mind was not perturbed by the noise and became tranquil. He felt ebullient and at ease, with this feeling enveloping his whole body. He called this feeling *pītisukham* or elation and bliss[10]. However, his mind was still focused on awareness with silent inner talk of his in-breath and out-breath.

The Buddha later categorized the state of elation and bliss (*pītisukham*) which he attained while practicing the awareness-of-the-breath method as the first samādhi stage. He stressed that being secluded from desires[11] and secluded from unwholesome states[12] were two fundamental conditions for attaining the state of elation and bliss using the *awareness-with-silent-talk* breathing method. These two elements were essential to the Buddha's awareness-of-the-breathing method.

Opening a new path

The Bodhisattva tried to re-apply his breathing method to see whether applying it with the intention of rediscovering the state of *elation and bliss* would have the same result as what he experienced as a child. If this was the case, he would apply this method to attain a pure and peaceful mind that would lead to enlightenment and liberation.

He saw that by maintaining awareness of the gentle breathing in and out, he was indeed able to attain the state of *elation and bliss* just like when he was a child, although his mind still had inner talk (*vitakka*) and inner dialogue (*vicāra*).

He was delighted to discover that his mind was pure and devoid of desires just like when he was a child. This was the result of his six years of effort against the demands of the senses. His mind had become impregnable. The body's habit of craving pleasures no longer had the power to pressure his mind into satisfying its demands.

When he was a child, his mind was totally pure. It had not acquired the habit of passionately wanting pleasures and did not carry malicious, cruel thoughts against any living creatures. Likewise, his mind was now also totally pure: free of desires and defilements; unafraid of hunger, pain, scorching sun, rain, cold; devoid of malice and cruelty toward any living beings; free from attachment to any objects. He had reached this state despite having spent his whole life prior to his renunciation deep in passion toward worldly pleasures, consuming as his senses dictated and engrossed in the luxury and magnificence of his princely life. He realized that this was the fruit of the six years spent in harrowing self-mortification practice.

Drawing lessons from the Buddha's experience

In examining the Buddha's activities during his six years of strenuous self-mortification practice and living in isolation in the forest, we can conclude that, in regard to seclusion from desires, he was freed from the five categories of desires:

1. Money and material wealth.

2. Attraction to the other sex.

3. Fame, good reputation, honors and compliments.

4. Good tasting food, interesting and luxury items.

5. Resting in high beds with comfortable mattresses and warm blankets.

He gained complete control of his senses and consumed only as needed, free from desires. He was at all times watchful about the lapses of his mind and intellect and about not letting his senses be influenced by their objects.

CHAPTER 2: THE INVALUABLE EXPERIENCE 97

He recognized that the mind and intellect are the original causes of sorrow.

In regard to seclusion from unwholesome states, over nearly six years he eschewed lust, killing, stealing, lying, derisive speech, encouraging discontent, embellishing the truth, not telling the whole truth, talking oneself up and putting others down. Nor did he harbor anger, hatred, unwholesome views, or slandering thoughts. He had also completely attained true *loving-kindness* toward all living beings, especially the insects that live on the ground, and true *equanimity* such as when the cowherd boys viciously poked sticks into his ears, urinated and threw rubbish onto him.

These were two invaluable experiences.

The new discovery

The Buddha's experiences with the breathing meditation practice of his youth had been committed to his long term memory, or in Zen Buddhism terminology, had been **subsumed into his wordless cognition**. This was the reason why, when he reapplied it, he attained immediately a tranquil state of mind and felt elation and bliss arising in him. The new discovery was indeed a **condensed cognition**[13] about the breathing method.

This was a most important pre-condition which determined his success when he progressed through stages one, two, three and finally stage four of samādhi without meeting any obstacles.

Those of us who are beginners in Buddhist meditation, and are yet to experience the tranquility of mind that the Bodhisattva had, need to create more favorable preconditions by assiduously practicing over a long period of time in order to silence the inner talk and inner dialogue, and terminate our attachment to feelings and sensations of elation and bliss.

The Buddha would later establish the foundations of the first stage of meditation. Those who wish to successfully complete the first stage of meditation need to maintain adequate discipline, live with true morality, maintain control of the six senses, and keep the mind and intellect free of their tendencies to embellish. He was very pleased to see that the path toward enlightenment and liberation could start with the breathing method built on the principles of seclusion from desires, seclusion from unwholesome states and **single-thought awareness** with silent talk of the in-breath and out-breath, by maintaining an awareness assisted by silent talk of each in-breath and out-breath.

This was a new discovery. Although he had made this discovery when he was a young child, he had not paid attention to it in the following 20 years. He did not pay attention to it in his previous two spiritual journeys, instead seeking things that came from outside – things that he would later call "the Born". Now that he was at a complete impasse, he remembered it. He realized that the feeling of elation and bliss (*pītisukham*) arose from the absence of attachment to worldly pleasures, and the absence of malicious and immoral acts and thoughts toward others. He then asked himself the question: *"Is this the path that leads to enlightenment?"*

Following this thought, inside his holy mind the answer arose: *"This is the path that leads to enlightenment"*.

He still prudently raised a question as to whether he needed to "fear" this pleasant feeling, that is, whether he would get attached to the pleasant feeling if he enjoyed it. He asked himself: *"Do I fear this pleasant feeling that arises from the seclusion from desires and from unwholesome states?"*

The answer came back from within his pure mind: *"I do not fear this pleasant feeling".*

He need not "fear" it because this was the result of his determined struggle against the demands and cravings of the body, through exerting maximal control over his six senses and not letting them become attached to the six objects of the senses, as well as always keeping his mind in a state of clear awareness.

He recounted to Aggivessana:

Then, Aggivessana, I thought: 'I recall that when my father the Sakyan was occupied, while I was sitting in the cool shade of a rose-apple[14] tree, quite secluded from desires, secluded from unwholesome states — I entered upon and abided in the first meditation[15] which is accompanied by inner talk and inner dialogue[16], with elation and bliss born of seclusion. Could that be the path to enlightenment? Then, following on that memory, came the realization: 'That is the path to enlightenment'.

Then, Aggivessana, I thought: 'Why am I afraid of that pleasant feeling[17] that has nothing to do with desires and unwholesome states?' I thought: 'I am not afraid of that pleasant feeling since it has nothing to do with desires and unwholesome states.' (Majjhima Nikāya (The Middle Length Discourses of the Buddha"), Mahāsaccaka Sutta, "The Greater Discourse to Saccaka", sutta #36, MN 36:32 and MN 36:33)

The dawn of enlightenment had truly started to appear.

Starting the Middle Path

Looking at his terribly emaciated body and his wrecked state of health, the Bodhisattva realized that he could not start his long journey to attain enlightenment in such miserable bodily and near-death conditions. He recognized the errors in the practice of torturing the body and his past determination in inflicting suffering onto himself. He thought that he should resume normal eating to rebuild his health and stop putting in maximal effort to inflict suffering onto himself. He considered that the body was a precious vehicle that he could lean on during his spiritual journey. No matter how strong his mind was, he would fail on his spiritual journey if his body was exhausted.

The Middle Path doctrine started from that time.

This was the Bodhisattva's third awakening and the most crucial change in direction on his spiritual journey before attaining enlightenment.

The Buddha would later further develop the concept of the Middle Path in several sermons on abolishing extreme opposite positions on any subjects. In this way, Buddhism would not take sides. The school of Developmental Buddhism further developed the doctrine into Non-Dualism or Neither-Existing-nor-Non-Existing. Or, as Venerable Nāgārjuna said: "The Middle Path has no position."

REFERENCES
FOR CHAPTER II
Section 3

SUTTAS

1. Kinh Trung Bộ (Majjhima Nikāya) – Translated into Vietnamese by Hòa Thượng Thích Minh Châu, Saigon, 1986, pp. 179-188 and pp. 531-539

2. The Middle Length Discourses of the Buddha – A New Translation of the Majjhima Nikāya – Translated by Bhikkhu Ñāṇamoli and Bhikkhu Bodhi, Wisdom Publications, Boston, 1995, MN 12:44 to MN 12:64, MN 36:12 to MN 36:32

COMMENTARIES

3. Buddhist Scriptures, by Edward Conze, England, 1959, pp. 45-48.

4. The Life of Buddha, by A. Ferdinand Herold, Tokyo, Japan, 1954, pp. 72-78.

5. The Gospel of Buddha, by Paul Carus, London, 1995, pp. 34-35.

6. The Buddha and His Dhamma, by Dr. B.R. Ambedkar, Taiwan, 1997, pp. 61-67.

7. The Buddha and His Teachings, by Mahāthera Nārada, Sri Lanka, 1964, pp. 6-7; 14-17.

8. An Introduction to Buddhism, by Peter Harvey, England, 1990, pp. 21-22.

9. The Living Thoughts of Gotama the Buddha, by Ananda K. Coomaraswamy and I. B. Horner, New Delhi - India, 1981, pp. 44-45.

10. Buddhism in Translations, by Henry C. Warren, New Delhi, 1986, pp. 48-49.

CHAPTER III

THE DECISIVE STAGE

1

THE THIRD JOURNEY:

THE MIDDLE PATH AND THE PROCESS OF SPIRITUAL REALIZATION

Introduction

After six years of brutal self-mortification practice – which resulted in an emaciated body with only skin over bones, and also in his losing consciousness – the Bodhisattva was saved by the sheep's milk offered by a young shepherdess and slowly regained consciousness. He realized that his first priority was to eat normally again to regain his strength.

Reviewing previous practices

A few days later, the Bodhisattva reflected on his near six years of self-mortification practice and concluded that he had made the following mistakes:

- He had blindly accepted traditional beliefs and the expected results of self-mortification as described by Koṇḍañña. Not until he lost all physical strength and nearly died did he recognize his mistake in believing someone else's claims even though he had **not seen, known and put them into practice**. This was blind faith and not the conviction of an intelligent person.

- A strong determination is necessary on the spiritual journey toward higher wisdom and *Nibbāna*, but if it is not combined with the **correct practice method**, it can

CHAPTER 3: THE DECISIVE STAGE

become an obstacle. One should recognize that the practice method, and not the amount of effort put into the practice, is the most crucial factor. One's **strong will must be used in the right place alongside a correct practice method.**

- A brutal self-mortification practice could eradicate desires and unwholesome conduct, but it also resulted in an exhausted body and an agitated mind, incapable of sustaining simple movements and thinking clearly due to the ravage of hunger. The Bodhisattva realized that only with a healthy body and a sufficiently sated stomach could one make progress in the spiritual practice. If the body is exhausted and ravaged by hunger, the mind cannot attain the tranquility required for spiritual practice. The Bodhisattva realized that the doctrine of mortifying the body to *vanquish and master the mind* was doomed to failure. The body is a vehicle that the mind leans on in one's spiritual practice. On the path to enlightenment and liberation, if one neglects, tortures, oppresses excessively, and enfeebles the body, how can the mind continue practicing? On the other hand, if the mind becomes enamored with the five desires and focuses on satisfying the sensual demands of the body, the body will reap dire consequences, which results eventually in the ruin of both body and mind. Consequently, body and mind must be in harmony for spiritual practice to reach the desired outcome.

- At that point, he considered that the body had an important role to play. Self-mortification had run its course and he would no longer mortify his body. He would resume eating normally to recover his strength.

This opinion would later become the Buddha's Middle Path doctrine: *not excessive self-mortification, but also not excessive self-indulgence.*

Upholding transparency and righteousness

Once he had recovered his health, the Bodhisattva went from the caves in the Mahākāḷa Mountains to the Phalgu River where the five ascetic monks were staying. He told them that he had abandoned self-mortification and had resumed eating normally to regain his strength.

He asserted that self-mortification not only did not help him attain his goal but nearly caused his death. That was why he would no longer practice self-mortification and would resume eating normally to maintain good health and use the body as a vehicle that the mind could lean on in order to practice. As for a practice method, he would apply the breathing method that he had experienced in his youth. He would inform the five monks once he reached his objective.

Leaving in disapproval

The five ascetic monks were angry when they heard that the Bodhisattva had abandoned the spiritual practice that they revered and had taught him. They considered that he no longer deserved their assistance since he had adopted a lifestyle of luxury and self-indulgence and had abandoned a practice which was consistent with a holy life and vindicated by tradition. They despised him, left him on his own and went to Isipatana.

Proof through success

The Bodhisattva knew that the Koṇḍañña group misconceived the path to enlightenment by blindly putting their faith in the traditional self-mortification method. He was not concerned by their stubbornness in holding on to an erroneous tradition, nor their protest nor the disdain that they showed toward him.

He was full of compassion for them but felt no need to explain himself further or rectify their incorrect assessment of his character. All he needed to do was to succeed and show them the wisdom of abandoning the traditional practice of extreme self-mortification.

The Buddha continued to tell the story to Aggivessana:

Then, Aggivessana, I considered: 'It is not easy to attain that bliss with a body so excessively emaciated. Suppose I ate some solid food – some boiled rice and bread.' And then I ate some solid food – some boiled rice and bread. Now at that time five Bhikkhus were waiting upon me, thinking: 'If our recluse Gotama achieves some higher state, he will inform us.' But when I ate the boiled rice and bread, the five Bhikkhus were disgusted and left me, thinking: 'The recluse Gotama now lives luxuriously; he has given up his striving and reverted to luxury.' (Majjhima Nikāya, "The Middle Length Discourses of the Buddha", Sutta #36, Mahāsaccaka Sutta, "The Greater Discourse to Saccaka", MN 36:33)

Leaving the self-mortification forest

After his five co-practitioners had left, the Bodhisattva also left the self-mortification forest. A forest on the other side of the Phalgu River, where many banyan (*ajapāla*) trees grew, seemed to him a good choice of place to stay and practice his sitting meditation.

After that, he crossed the Phalgu River. It was then around March or April of our current calendar and the river would have been quite shallow. The Phalgu River is currently about 1,000 meters wide.

The banyan (ajapāla) tree

CHAPTER 3: THE DECISIVE STAGE

Every day, the Bodhisattva went into a nearby village to beg for food. This village was called Senānīgama, the village of the wealthy landowner Senānī who was the father of a young woman named Sujātā. The village lay between the Phalgu and the Nerañjara rivers which are tributaries of

The shallow Phalgu River in winter. On each side of the river are sandbanks. On the other side of the river, in the Buddha's days, there was a banyan tree forest. The land belonged to Mr. Senānī, the father of Sujātā

the Ganges (*Ganga*). They flow from a branch of the Ganges located at Dispur, in the town of Patna, state of Bihar.

The width of the village, which is the distance between the Phalgu and Nerañjara rivers, was about 2,000 meters.

The Bodhisattva then practiced the breathing method that he experienced when he was a child.

A wonderful assisting causal condition

Small temple that marks the place where the Bodhisattva received the offering of cake from Sujātā and Puññā. It is located about 1,500 meters from the bank of the Nerañjara River.

Sujātā had previously prayed to a god in the banyan tree forest to have a son. Her wish was realized and she wanted to repay her debt of gratitude to the god. She asked her servant Puññā to visit the banyan tree forest and check if a god had appeared. If he had, Puññā was to rush back and tell her so that she could bake a special cake as an offering to the god. Puññā walked through the forest and arrived at the river where she saw what looked like a deity sitting at the foot of a banyan tree. She immediately went back to inform Sujātā. Sujātā made a tray of *kheer* cake (made of ground sticky rice mixed with milk and sugar) as an offering to the god.

This was a wonderful and timely causal condition assisting the Bodhisattva's practice. With the help of this cake, over several weeks, the Bodhisattva did not need to spend time on obtaining food for his body and could assiduously focus on his practice. He eventually attained the goal that he had when he started his spiritual journey.

Choosing an environment to practice

After eating some cake, the Bodhisattva thought that this was the right time to put his effort into practicing the breathing method since he did not have to go begging for food. But his location was no longer suitable for a focused practice as it was frequented by people. He had previously gone to the other bank of the Nerañjara River (Nairañjanā in Sanskrit, today called the Nīlājanā) and knew that there were no people's houses and only an old forest there. He thought that this location was quieter and more suitable for a focused practice.

He made the decision to leave his current location, got up and started to walk briskly toward the old forest on the other side of the Nerañjara River.

When he was near the river bank, a grass cutter named Sotthīya offered him four bundles of *kusha* grass (this type of grass has long leaves much like lemongrass and grows in abundance along the Nerañjara River). He accepted the offering and crossed the river...

Banks of the Nerañjara River

Nowadays, in the holy site area, archeologists have erected two commemorative monuments: (1) a small temple located about 1500 meters from the Nerañjara River to mark the location where Sujātā and Puññā made the offering of cake to the Bodhisattva; next to this temple, there are *ajapāla* banyan trees; (2) a small stupa about 100 meters from the Nerañjara River to mark the location where the grass cutter offered the *kusha* grass to the Bodhisattva.

Realizing and abiding in the first meditation stage

After crossing the Nerañjara River, the Bodhisattva chose for his sitting meditation a site under an old *pipphala* (also called *pipal*) tree about 900 meters from the bank of the Nerañjara. This tree had a lush and broad canopy that would protect him from the sun and rain. (The Bodhisattva attained enlightenment under this *pipphala* tree, and this type of tree has since been called Bodhi[1] tree).

CHAPTER 3: THE DECISIVE STAGE 113

Kusha grass (left) and a small stupa (right), about 100 meters from the Nerañjara River, that marks the location where the grass cutter Sotthīya offered the kusha grass to the Bodhisattva

The Bodhisattva spread the *kusha* grass into a sitting mat, sat with his back to the *pipphala* tree and his face toward the Nerañjara River and made a vow:

Though only my skin, sinews, and bones remain, and my blood and flesh dry up and wither away, yet will I never stir from this seat until I have attained the supreme enlightenment[2].

According to the Mahāsaccaka Sutta ("The Greater Discourse to Saccaka") sutta #36 of the Majjhima Nikāya ("The Middle Length Discourses of the Buddha"), the Bodhisattva first learnt the Yoga method of meditation then abandoned this method to follow his own practice.

This was the beginning of a process that started with a breathing method that consisted of several practice steps. These steps led the Bodhisattva to a state of elation (*pīti*) and bliss (*sukha*), even though his mind still had inner talk and inner dialogue, in other words a state of *"elation and bliss with inner talk and inner dialogue"*. The Buddha called this state "samādhi with inner talk and inner dialogue." According to historical records, the Bodhisattva practiced this method for one week.

We don't know exactly how the Bodhisattva practiced, how many days he spent on each step, but we know from the Samyutta Nikāya, "The Connected Discourses of the Buddha", Book 5, Chapter 10 Ānāpānasamyutta "Connected Discourses on Breathing", vagga "One Thing", SN 54:1, that the Buddha taught disciples several steps in the breathing method.

For the first samādhi stage, the Buddha taught disciples to say silently: *"I know I am breathing in, I know I am breathing out…"*.

The focus of this step was "**awareness with silent inner talk**", with the silent inner talk being the silent talk that accompanied the in-breath and out-breath. The effect of awareness with silent inner talk is the severance of the old habit of chatter in the mind that arises from the *mind faculty, the consciousness and the intellect*. The mind of the practitioner starts to become serene, and s/he experiences elation and bliss. This is why awareness with silent inner talk is seen as a fundamental and effective instrument to calm the false mind. It was later categorized as equivalent to *samatha* (tranquility) meditation.

CHAPTER 3: THE DECISIVE STAGE

It is important to note that the silent inner talk must be associated with awareness, otherwise wandering thoughts will insert themselves into the mind.

Later, in his teaching, the Buddha would call this state "samādhi with inner talk and inner dialogue".

We should note that during this stage the Bodhisattva's body experienced a feeling of elation and bliss however this feeling did not influence his mind. The *pleasant feeling* remained separate from his mind. In this instance, the Bodhisattva's mind had started to play the role of "witness". It was quite exceptional that the Bodhisattva had managed to control the pleasant feeling from the very first week. This could be understood by recalling that the Bodhisattva had already achieved a high level of control from his days practicing self-mortification, but this control had not become a stable energy. This was why during the first three stages of meditation, the Bodhisattva's mind was still attached to feelings and sensations. He later recognized that this attachment was due to him still having some mental murmuring (*manojalpa*) about the pleasant feeling. By applying the technique of "silent awareness about the pleasant feeling" he became fully in control of his consciousness and went beyond the pleasant feeling.

He recounted to Aggivessana how the pleasant feeling arose but did not influence his mind:

Now, Aggivessana, when I had taken solid food and regained my strength, then quite secluded from desires, secluded from unwholesome states, I entered upon and abided in the first meditation, which is accompanied by inner talk and inner dialogue, with elation and bliss born of seclusion. But such pleasant feelings that arose in me did not invade my mind and remain. (MN 36:34)

Observations

- The Buddha's first stage of meditation shows that, by continuously being aware of the in-breath and out-breath, one can stop wandering thoughts from arising out of one's working memory, long term memory and emotional memory. These wandering thoughts agitate the mind faculty, the consciousness and the intellect. As they stop arising, the mind gradually becomes more still, less disturbed, and starts to become tamed. Under similar circumstances, one can experience elation and bliss permeating one's entire body.

- The Buddha called this state *"samādhi with inner talk and inner dialogue"* since he still applied silent talk to his breathing. The key to this technique is *verbal awareness*, also called single-thought awareness, where the content of the awareness is the in-breath and out-breath. The Buddha also classified this state as *"unified mind"*. This state is equivalent to "awareness" and is the foundation of the first stage of meditation or first stage of samādhi. The consciousness (*viññāṇa*) is inactive and the mind is not focused on the external world.

- Some ancient Buddhist Commentary Masters have identified five characteristics of the first stage of samādhi: inner talk (*vitakka*), inner dialogue (*vicāra*), elation (*pīti*), bliss (*sukha*), and one-pointedness of mind (*citassa-ekaggatā*). In this explanation, the consciousness is active and the mind focuses or concentrates on the object. This state is equivalent to "mindfulness".

Question: Master, could you please explain the difference between the "one-pointedness" samādhi and the "unified mind" samādhi?

CHAPTER 3: THE DECISIVE STAGE 117

Answer: One-pointedness-of-mind is a term found in the Compendium of States of Phenomena (*Dhamma-saṅgani*), a text that Venerable Mogalliputta Tissa recorded in the Commentaries (*Abhidhamma*) section of the Tipiṭaka during the third sutta-consolidating Buddhist Council convened under the reign of King Aśoka in the 3rd century BC. Later in the 5th century AD, or 800 years after the Buddha's death, in The Path of Purification Treatise (*Visuddhimagga*) Venerable Buddhagoṣa also gave prominence to the one-pointedness of mind as the state of samādhi. On the other hand, in the Nikāya, the Buddha gave prominence to the unified mind as the state of samādhi. These two models are in total opposition to each other.

The unified mind is attained through self-awareness whereas one-pointedness-of-mind is attained through the mind faculty, the consciousness and the intellect. These two concepts lead to different types of samādhi.

Question: Master, could you please explain in detail the differences between these two types of samādhi?

Answer: "One-pointedness-of-mind" requires the practitioner to concentrate his/her mind on one point. This has led many Western scholars to translate samādhi as "concentration". The subject doing the concentration is the "I/Me". To accomplish one-pointedness-of-mind requires the practitioner to focus his/her whole mind ("mindfulness") onto the object.

On the other hand, the "unified mind" requires the practitioner to apply his/her "awareness". In this way, samādhi is equivalent to the state of "wordless awareness" in which the subject being aware of the unified mind is the **capacity for self-awareness**.

The effects of these two concepts differ profoundly:

1. Achieving a stillness of mind through concentration will continuously activate the sympathetic nervous system which produces at its extremities the biochemical norepinephrine. This biochemical is a noxious substance that causes harm to the body and brain. Sustained practice of the concentration method can result in high blood pressure, diabetes and memory loss. Finally, this method will not lead to experiencing samādhi under the *tathā*-mind state.

2. Achieving a stillness of mind though the unified-mind method, which is based on wordless awareness, will activate the parasympathetic nervous system which produces at its extremities the biochemical acetylcholine. This substance helps bring the body into balance and generates a feeling of joy, also called **elation**. Once this feeling of elation becomes deeper, it triggers the hypothalamus into secreting the biochemical dopamine. The effect of dopamine is to generate a feeling of bliss in the mind.

By attaining **unified-mind** samādhi, the practitioner experiences a feeling of elation and bliss. This samādhi will take the practitioner to the ultimate destination which is the *tathā*-mind.

These are the profound differences between the two forms of samādhi.

Realizing and abiding in the second meditation stage

During the first meditation stage, the Bodhisattva experienced a sense of elation and bliss permeating his entire body. He felt that his mind was tranquil and pure. He

CHAPTER 3: THE DECISIVE STAGE

recognized that this was mainly due to its seclusion from desires and unwholesome states. However, he could not attain a deeper level of tranquility as inner talk (*vitakka*) and inner dialogue (*vicāra*) continued to alternately arise in his mind. The Bodhisattva then progressed to the second stage that terminated the inner talk and inner dialogue.

In the second stage, he no longer exerted effort in using his consciousness or his intellect to contemplate, memorize, monitor and direct his in-breath and out-breath through the silent talk: "I know I am taking a long in-breath", "I know I am taking a long out-breath", as he did previously. His breath came in and out naturally, and he just maintained a *clear awareness of his in-breath and out-breath*. There was only awareness, and no one being aware. He called it "right awareness of the in-breath, right awareness of the out-breath". Later, he taught his disciples: "Taking in a long breath, this person is **clearly aware**: 'I am taking in a long breath'. Taking in a short breath, this person is **clearly aware**: 'I am taking in a short breath'". The practitioner maintains a **clear awareness** while breathing in and breathing out without adding any further content to it. This clear awareness is equivalent to the state of **silent awareness**.

This is the technique of "being aware of the object" by *bare attention* or *bare observation* of the breathing-in and breathing-out. There is no subject being aware, there is only the awareness of the breathing-in and breathing-out.

For example, when we breathe in, we are *clearly aware* of the in-breath; when we breathe-out, we are *clearly aware* of the out-breath: when taking in a long breath, we are *clearly aware* of taking a long breath; when breathing out a long breath, we are *clearly aware* of breathing out a long breath.

When the abdomen inflates, we are *clearly aware* of the abdomen inflating; when the abdomen deflates, we are *clearly aware* of the abdomen deflating. There is a *clear awareness* of the activities associated with the breathing-in and breathing-out. In this clear awareness, there is no silent talk about the inflating or deflating of the abdominal muscles, of the rib cage or the diaphragm. Nor is the consciousness present to differentiate the states of shortness, length, depth, shallowness, coarseness, subtleness, or purity of the breath. Adding any silent talk into this process would go against the nature of the **samādhi without inner talk and inner dialogue**.

The practitioner has a clear awareness of the in-breath and out-breath, whether it is coarse, subtle, long, short, deep or shallow, but this *awareness is without silent talk about itself*, and is only a silent awareness. It involves knowing the in-breath and out-breath as they are. There is no subject I/Me knowing, there is only a clear awareness. This is the **self-awareness** that is innate to the ultimate touch function of the **wordless awareness mind**.

By using this method, the Bodhisattva's mind became clear, tranquil and clearly aware of the sensations from his body. A feeling of elation and bliss permeated his entire body, caused by biochemicals secreted by the endocrine system. He enjoyed this state and continued to maintain this feeling of elation and bliss. However, he also became less motivated to progress further.

The Bodhisattva re-assessed his mind to understand the reason for this obstacle. Finally, he identified the inner talk (*vitakka*) that emerged in response to the feeling of elation and bliss as the source of the obstacle. He considered this an illness[*]. He then endeavored to terminate the *inner talk* by not responding to the feeling of elation and bliss. Subsequently, both inner talk and inner dialogue (*vicāra*) became silent. (This is called "eliminating inner talk and inner dialogue" in the suttas). All that remained was a *clear awareness of the in-breath and out-breath* without any person being aware. He identified this state as "samādhi without inner talk and inner dialogue".

The Bodhisattva continued to practice this step many more times until he was totally in control of his chattering mind, achieving a state of inner serenity with a mind devoid of wandering thoughts (this state is called "inner serenity with unity of mind[3]" in the suttas). At that time, although the feeling of elation and bliss permeated his entire body, and although he was very clearly aware of this state, his mind did not become attached to it. His mind had truly reached the state of samādhi (*samādhiyati*).

He thus recounted his realization and abiding in the second stage of meditation to Aggivessana:

With the stilling of inner talk and inner dialogue, I entered upon and abided in the second meditation: elation and bliss born of stillness, unification of awareness free from inner talk and inner dialogue - internal assurance. But such pleasant feeling that arose in me did not invade my mind and remain. (MN 36:35)

NOTE

In the Samyutta Nikāya, "The Connected Discourses of the Buddha", Samyutta 54 Ānāpānasamyutta "Connected

---

[*] This is mentioned in the Aṅguttara Nikāya, "The Numerical Discourses of the Buddha", Book of Fours, pp. 200-201

Discourses on Breathing", vagga "One Thing", SN 54:8, the Buddha said that before he attained the Full Enlightenment, he often applied the technique of "samādhi with awareness of the in-breath and out-breath". He said that on multiple occasions he practiced the breathing method with "*sati-samādhi*", or samādhi with awareness, and this kept his body and eyes from ever being tired. This means that when he reached this state, he did not feel slothful or lethargic. His mind was not influenced by mental defilements and was not attached to the objects of the senses. He said:

It is in this way, Bhikkhus, that awareness samādhi of breathing is developed and cultivated so that it is of great fruit and benefit.

I too, Bhikkhus, before my enlightenment, while I was still a Bodhisattva, not yet fully enlightened, generally dwelt in this place. While I generally dwelt in this place, neither my body nor my eyes became fatigued and my mind, by not clinging, was liberated from defilements.

From this experience, the Buddha later developed the "Awareness of breathing-in and breathing-out samādhi" method to teach disciples the path to attain the second meditation stage or *samādhi without inner talk and inner dialogue* state.

He identified several practice steps within this method, of which the two most important consist of stopping thoughts and completely stopping inner talk and inner dialogue. This is the most important samādhi stage in Buddhist meditation, since it is only once one has attained it that one can control one's chattering mind and thinking process. This is the required condition before progressing deeper into other stages of samādhi. If the verbal chattering in our mind is not kept under control, we cannot control our wandering thoughts and experience samādhi.

Also in the Samyutta Nikāya, SN 54:8, the Buddha said: *Therefore, Bhikkhus, if a bhikkhu wishes: 'May the memories and intentions connected with household life be abandoned by me', this same awareness samādhi of breathing should be closely attended to*[4].

The Buddha went on to describe how the "awareness samādhi of breathing-in and breathing-out" leads to the *elimination of inner talk and inner dialogue*:

Therefore, Bhikkhus, if a bhikkhu wishes: 'May I, with the subsiding of inner talk and inner dialogue, enter and dwell in the second meditation, which has inner serenity and unity of mind, is without inner talk and inner dialogue, and has elation and bliss born of stillness', this same awareness samādhi of breathing should be closely attended to.

Meaning of Awareness Samādhi "Sati-samādhi"

- The Pāli term *"sati"* here does not mean "to remember" but *"awareness"*. Therefore *"sati samādhi"* does not mean "samādhi through remembering" but *"samādhi through awareness"*. This means that, at this stage, the awareness has become a stable energy. Within this awareness, the false mind is absent and only a wordless awareness[5] remains. This is what the Buddha meant by "awareness samādhi". Understanding *"sati"* as "to remember" would be incorrect.

For example, when we breathe in, we are *aware* that we are breathing in. When we breathe out, we are *aware* that we are breathing out. When our abdomen rises with the in-breath, we are *aware* of the rising; when our abdomen sinks with the out-breath, we are *aware* of the sinking. There is awareness, and nothing else. This awareness is very clear and without interruption. There is no verbal chattering in the mind about any subject. This awareness is not a *knowing by the consciousness* but is a *silent awareness*. To use Zen Buddhist terminology, the former is the knowing by the consciousness whereas the latter is the knowing by the wordless awareness mind. In this awareness, there is no one being aware, there is only a silent flow of awareness about the in-breath, out-breath and every other objects. This is *knowing-things-as-they-are*. From a neuroscience perspective, this is a state of **self-awareness by ultimate touch**.

- The Buddha maintained a *silent awareness* of the in-breath and out-breath but did not focus his mind on controlling his breath. Nor did he have thoughts to differentiate how the in-breath and out-breath were, whether they were long or short, rapid or slow… In this way, the old habit of inner talk (*vitakka*) and inner dialogue (*vicāra*) could not automatically arise. In this process of breathing-in and breathing-out, the verbal chattering cannot suddenly insert itself into the mind, and what remains in the mind is just the *awareness* of the in-breath and out-breath.

Effects of awareness samādhi

- When *awareness samādhi* has become an ever present energy, both inner talk and inner dialogue have obviously become silent since it is they that constitute the silent verbal chattering in our mind. Inner talk and inner dialogue are two major obstacles in the early stages of samādhi meditation practice discussed under several other topics of Buddhist meditation. *Awareness samādhi* is an awareness that has become permanent, stable and uninterrupted. It represents the second stage of samādhi, in which the mind remains in a state of silent awareness where the consciousness, the mind faculty and the intellect are all absent.

- When the Buddha achieved control of the *inner talk and inner dialogue*, his mind became completely tranquil. He experienced a feeling of elation and bliss enveloping his body. He knew that this state was caused by the state of *samādhi without inner talk and inner dialogue* and not by seclusion from desires and unwholesome states. However, the pleasant feeling endured, and occasionally an *inner talk* would arise in his mind to note the impression made by the pleasant feeling. He considered this inner talk an illness. He subsequently decided that he needed to eliminate all inner talk in order for the mind to be detached from the pleasant feeling. He eventually overcame the obstacle. He was still aware of the pleasant feeling but it did not influence his mind. Eventually, when he reached the third stage of meditation, the pleasant feeling became extinct.

Observations

- It is very difficult for the ordinary person to attain the state of samādhi without inner talk and inner dialogue because the habit of thinking and ideation has been entrenched in the three components of one's worldly mind – the consciousness, mind faculty and intellect – since one reached the age of 10 months or so.

- By contrast, the Buddha had lived many years in isolation in the remote forest. He did not have idle thoughts, did not dwell in the past, did not discuss worldly pleasures or have disputes with other people. Instead, he concentrated his efforts onto fighting greed and desires. When he recognized that inner talk and inner dialogue still appeared in his mind, he put his effort into controlling the speech formation process. He eventually reached his objective.

Points to note

- If we have been practicing meditation for many years but still cannot stop wandering thoughts from arising in our mind, we may have fallen prey to the following shortcomings: (1) not recognizing the root causes of the wandering thoughts; (2) not being able to control the muttering in the mind, that is the mental murmur (*manojalpa*); (3) not recognizing the danger of inner talk and inner dialogue in impeding the level of samādhi attained and strengthening mental defilements; (4) not attaining samādhi without inner talk and inner dialogue.

- In reality, *inner talk and inner dialogue* constitute our wandering thoughts, which are caused by our mind being attracted to objects through the action of the consciousness. It is the consciousness that causes the ceaseless attachment to objects. The essence of wandering thoughts is the ceaseless verbal chattering or the constant silent inner dialogue in our mind. They are real. They are caused by us starting an inner conversation or they arise due to the habit of verbal chattering in our mind. Our inner mind is like a sea agitated by the waves created by the chattering mind. The dense web of thoughts in our mind is woven by the chattering in our mind. We can eradicate these thoughts by applying techniques to control the chattering mind. If we can control our chattering mind, we will be able to

CHAPTER 3: THE DECISIVE STAGE 127

experience samādhi in all four postures, i.e. in our everyday activities. Otherwise, even if we use contemplation to reason with ourselves that our wandering thoughts are falsehoods and delusions, they will still remain present in our mind. They will continue to lead us astray, and our meditation practice will come to an impasse. This is why we need to recognize the source and true nature of wandering thoughts and then apply the right method to eliminate them.

- If a person does not experience the state of samādhi without inner talk and inner dialogue, his/her mind will continue to be filled with wandering thoughts. S/he is then susceptible to one day being led into judgmental entanglement and perversion by the past-present-future mind.

Understanding the value of the second stage of meditation

Based on the Bodhisattva's achievement in the second stage of meditation, we can draw out eight key points that will help our understanding of this stage:

1. **The essence of samādhi without inner talk and inner dialogue**: the ultimate core meaning of the term "without inner talk and inner dialogue" is "without thinking," "without discursive thinking" or "without silent talk and silent dialogue in the mind". Consequently, the Feelings and Sensations and Perception aggregates cannot arise because Perception has come under the control of the wordless awareness mind, which causes the mind to be free of attraction to objects and reasoning, observing and thinking about them.

2. Please note the function of the Perception (*saññā*) aggregate. Perception is manifested through many forms of energies that all result in inner talk.

These energies are associated with "naming", "conceptualizing", "thought formation", "impression formation" and "association". Perception is always linked with what we experience in our daily life. When the six senses come into contact with the environment around us, naming, conceptualizing, thought formation, etc. immediately arise. For example, when we see an object, our Perception immediately describes it, associates a name to it, etc. The information generated by Perception's networks is then sent to the Mental Formation aggregate and to the Consciousness aggregate.

Through this process, our mind is like a moving tide and never stays still. The Buddha has experienced this fact and taught us to let go of the feeling of elation and bliss during the various stages of meditation. If we remain attached to our feelings and sensations, the speech formation process will be triggered without fail. When the speech formation process is really silenced, we will experience the state of samādhi without inner talk and inner dialogue. Under this state of samādhi without inner talk and inner dialogue, we silently experience all feelings and sensations without being attached to them.

We need to note this point.

3. A person who has managed to maintain a stable *wordless awareness* or *silent awareness* state has also attained the state of samādhi without inner talk and inner dialogue. S/he is in control of his/her perceptual

CHAPTER 3: THE DECISIVE STAGE 129

patterns, an important step toward achieving the state of "witness". Those who practice meditation in the four postures of walking, standing, lying and sitting but use some technique of incessantly talking to themselves will not be able to progress to samādhi. The Buddha called this state "meditation illness" or "suffering". They should reevaluate their meditation practice with a clear mind. If they do not change, they will forever tread water and will not be able to attain samādhi.

4. **Mandatory requirement**: we must control our mental murmur in order to attain the state of samādhi without inner talk and inner dialogue. To do so we need to practice step by step the technique to control our mental murmur.

5. **Practice method**: there are two ways to attain this state of samādhi:

   (a) The first method consists of controlling the silent talking in our mind by one of the following techniques: "not naming objects" or "stopping verbal chattering in the mind".

   If we do not manage to control the silent talking in our mind, our perception function will be continuously activated. It will generate wandering thoughts in many different forms that will keep our mind disturbed and attached. Once we have steadily controlled our chattering mind we will attain the second stage of samādhi without needing to follow the Awareness-of-Breathing-In-and-Breathing-Out-Samādhi method.

   (b) If we follow the Awareness-of-Breathing-In-and-Breathing-Out-Samādhi method, we should practice without any silent talking about the breath. We should not say silently "I know I am breathing in...I know I am breathing out...", nor "count the breath from one to ten", nor "observe whether the in-breath and out-breath is long or short, shallow or deep, rough or subtle". When breathing, we only maintain a *wordless awareness* of the in-breath and out-breath and a *silent awareness* of the feelings and sensations that arise in our body. These techniques are called "bare attention" or "bare observation". This is how we control our perception function. Our sense organs, in particular our body and mind, continue to come into contact with objects and are aware of objects, but our mind does not silently discuss them. If we practice consistently in this way, we will attain the state of samādhi without inner talk and inner dialogue. We will also build the foundation of the third stage of meditation.

6. **Inner serenity and unified mind**: what is called *inner serenity and unified mind* in Buddhist texts is a characteristic of the state of samādhi without inner talk and inner dialogue. When we have attained this state, the serenity that is inside our wordless awareness mind (inner serenity) arises and we immediately experience an un-interrupted **flow of wordless awareness**. This is the state called "inner serenity and unified mind when the chattering mind is totally silent". Inside this mind, there is no disturbance by sundry thoughts and no wandering thoughts, but only a "single-thought awareness". This single-thought awareness is a stable, permanent and silent flow of wordless awareness. It is the foundation of samādhi.

CHAPTER 3: THE DECISIVE STAGE 131

Zen Buddhism describes this state of mind as the "self" being integrated with the wordless awareness mind into a unified whole. In this state, there is no concept of "self" but only a permanent, silent, and wordless awareness. This is a state of **self-awareness** – a function of the wordless awareness mind.

7. **Comparison**: the state of **thoughtlessness** mentioned in Zen Buddhism is equivalent to the state of samādhi without inner talk and inner dialogue. Because in thoughtlessness there is no thought that arises from the intellect, mind faculty or the consciousness but only a clear awareness of the external and inner environments at that moment in time. In that state of samādhi, there is only a flow of wordless awareness in the mind of the practitioner. The practitioner has a sense of inner calm and a clear experience of being not attached to duality, called the "unified mind".

8. **Pleasant feelings and sensations not influencing the mind**: this is a characteristic of the second stage of meditation. The Buddha said that *pleasant feelings arose and stayed in his mind, but did not influence his mind.*

This means that the Buddha's mind was not attached to the pleasant feelings because he did not silently talk about these feelings when he became *aware of them permeating his entire body*. This was why pleasant feelings arose in his body but did not influence his mind.

We know that the Perception aggregate generates ideation networks when it receives information or stimuli from the Feelings and Sensations aggregate. Once we are in control of the silent verbal chattering in our mind, our perception no longer influences our mind even though we have feelings and sensations of what we perceive. We can consider that the stimulus stops at the Feelings and Sensations aggregate. This results in us being only *silently aware* of the pleasant feelings.

The mind of the Buddha had reached the state of being a "witness". Even though he was aware of pleasant feelings arising in his body, he did not pursue them.

The above eight points characterize the second stage of samādhi.

Summary

1. Terminating inner talk and inner dialogue will result in a sense of elation and bliss that envelops the entire body and mind. This feeling of elation and bliss continues to pervade all our activities in the four postures. If we are not aware of it, we will wish to abide in the feeling of bliss to enjoy it, and as a result *inner talk* will arise to expound on the degree of bliss. We will then fall into a state of *samādhi with inner talk and without inner dialogue*. If we know that the feeling of elation and bliss is the normal consequence of keeping the chattering mind under control, we will not feel a liking for it nor will we be enamored with it. On the contrary, we will simply maintain a **silent awareness** and will eventually attain the third samādhi stage of Equanimity. Our mind will become tranquil, balanced, devoid of joy or sadness, of elation, bliss, or attachment. The main content during this state of **equanimity** is the state of "No Talk".

2. Once one is able to maintain a steady second stage of meditation, then one will experience clarity of mind and

gain control of feelings and sensations, and emotions cannot arise. This is the foundation of the state of Equanimity or Full-and-Clear-Awareness-Samādhi (*Sati-sampajañña-samādhi*). In this state, the intellect, mind faculty, consciousness and ego are all inactive. This state brings the body and mind into harmony. The speech formation[6] process no longer runs in automatic mode following the old habits imprinted in brain cells in the memory and speech areas[7]. The Perception aggregate becomes truly silent. Our cognitive awareness emerges and becomes a witness.

This is a state called the **unified mind** (*cetaso-ekodhibhāva*). It is the basis for spiritual realization or inner realization[8]. The meditator perceives the transformations that occur in his/her body and mind but is not attached to these phenomena. Spiritual development is built on that basis.

However, because at this stage control of verbal chattering is not yet stable, the meditator will experience a sense of well-being permanently permeating his/her entire body. A permanent sense of joy reflects on his/her eyes and face and an innocent smile graces his/her face. If one does not know how to let go of this state of well-being or elation and bliss and continues to abide in it, this will become an "illness" because verbal chattering will find ground to resurface to enjoy the feeling of elation and bliss. This will prevent our progress toward the state of Equanimity which is the third stage of meditation. We should not abide in this feeling of elation and bliss but should remain deep in the state of samādhi without inner talk and inner dialogue in order to consolidate our self-awareness faculty which is our wordless awareness mind. We should not become attached to these feelings, sensations and perceptions.

3. **Necessary conditions for a successful practice**:

- First of all, when we practice, we need to clearly understand that the state of no inner talk and no inner dialogue (as mentioned in the Nikāya texts), or the state of no perception and no contemplation (as mentioned in the Āgama texts) means that there is no silent talk or silent back and forth dialogue in our mind about the topic of our meditation. At this stage, if verbal chattering still arises continuously in our mind while we meditate on any topic, we will be forever stuck at the first stage and cannot progress to the second stage.

- Second, we need to clearly understand that the essence of wordless awareness is awareness of an object through seeing, hearing or touch without any silent talk about that object. In this instance, the object of our awareness is the breathing-in and breathing-out. When we breathe in and out, if our body has feelings and sensations about the breathing, we do not say or think any silent word about these feelings and sensations but are only silently aware of them. We are practicing incorrectly if any silent thoughts arise in our mind, because thoughts activate the networks that constitute the perception aggregate. Consciousness, intellect, ego and mental factors will immediately manifest themselves, and the wordless awareness mind will evidently be absent. So we should remember: "never say anything silently, even if they are words to describe that our breath is tranquil and pure like a diamond". We only maintain a *silent awareness of the object or event*, or a clear awareness of the object or event without any representation or imagining about the breath. In this way, we practice in accordance with the awareness method that the Buddha taught.

- Third, we need to master the techniques for controlling the chattering mind, by applying bare attention or bare observation of the in-breath and out-breath. These techniques do not involve using the consciousness to focus attention on the topic or using the intellect to reason about the object. We only maintain a wordless awareness of the in-breath and out-breath, their length/shortness, depth/shallowness etc.

Realizing and abiding in the third meditation stage

After he attained a stable state of samādhi without inner talk and inner dialogue, the Bodhisattva experienced a continuous feeling of elation and bliss in all four postures. At this point he recognized that he needed to avoid this feeling of elation and bliss in order to advance to a higher level of meditation. If he continued to abide in the feeling of elation and bliss, his attention to it would continue to arise. He considered this state to be an illness.

He compared it to the situation of a person falling from utter happiness to suffering, and considered this suffering to be an illness[*].

He continued to go deeper in the **silent awareness** of the state of samādhi without inner talk and inner dialogue so that there was no verbal chattering attached to the feeling of

---

[*] In the Aṅguttara Nikāya, "The Numerical Discourses of the Buddha", Book of Nines, AN 9:41 "Tapussa", the Buddha said: "Sometime later, Ānanda, with the seclusion from elation… I entered and dwelled in the third meditation. While I was dwelling in this state, perception and attention accompanied by elation occurred in me and I felt it as an affliction"

elation, even though this feeling was present. The attachment to the feeling of elation subsequently became fainter and eventually vanished from his mind. He was "secluded from elation*" without exercising his will to be secluded from it.

He subsequently experienced a state of equanimity and serenity where his mind was no longer attached to any object, without any feeling of like or dislike.

He dwelled in this state of equanimity. (The suttas referred to this as *dwelling in equanimity*[9]. This means that he abided in a stable state of "No Talk".)

In this state of clear and wordless awareness, the Bodhisattva's body did not feel any tiredness and experienced an enveloping sense of bliss which resulted in an unperturbed mind. He later used specialized terms to indicate that the Holy Ones called this state of equanimity and abiding in all-enveloping bliss the "state of equanimity and awareness, dwelling in bliss, realizing and abiding in the third stage of meditation"†. However, although the feeling of bliss enveloped his entire body, it did not influence his mind, as at that point, he had attained "full and clear awareness"[10]. This is also the state of "**silent awareness of the no-talk state**".

The Buddha recounted to Aggivessana as follows:

---

* The Aṅguttara Nikāya, AN 9:41 "Tapussa", uses the term "seclusion from elation", the Madhyama Āgama, MĀ 44 "Discourse on Awareness" sutra, uses "seclusion from the sensual pleasure of elation", the Dīrgha Āgama, DĀ 20 "Ambattha" Sutra, uses "abandonment of elation"

† The Madhyama Āgama, MĀ 44 "Discourse on Awareness" sutra says: "What the holy ones declare equanimous and aware, dwelling in bliss stillness, realizing and abiding in the third stage of meditation, complete abiding".

CHAPTER 3: THE DECISIVE STAGE 137

Now, Aggivessana, with the seclusion from elation I remained equanimous, aware, and alert, and sensed bliss with the body. I entered upon and abided in the third meditation, of which the holy ones declare, 'equanimous and aware[11], he dwells in bliss[12].' But such pleasant feeling that arose and remain in me did not influence my mind. (MN 36:36)

This was the third time the Bodhisattva's mind had become filled with a stable wordless awareness energy. Even though a pleasant feeling permeated his entire body, it did not influence his mind.

To summarize, in the third stage of meditation, the Bodhisattva abandoned elation, abided in equanimity and experienced a feeling of bliss enveloping his entire body. However, a short time later he recognized that this state of bliss was an "illness" which he qualified as "suffering". If maintained, it would become an obstacle to progressing to the fourth stage of meditation. So, he continued to sink deeper into Equanimity to let go of *bliss*.

Eventually, he attained full and clear awareness which is a state of **clear and complete awareness** without any presence of verbal chattering in the mind in this process.

Understanding the value of the third stage of meditation

We can draw five important lessons from the Bodhisattva's success in the third stage of meditation:

1. **Abandoning elation**: this is the first method of the third meditation stage. Having attained the state of samādhi without inner talk and inner dialogue, the Bodhisattva experienced a feeling of elation enveloping his entire body. He subsequently noticed this feeling of elation

continuously appearing in his mind. He recognized that if he maintained this state, inner talk (*vitakka*) would have an opportunity to arise together with the feeling of *elation*. This would be an illness.

To terminate this illness, he continued to immerse himself deeper into the state of silent awareness of the state of samādhi without inner talk and inner dialogue. Shortly afterwards, the feeling of elation became progressively fainter and eventually ceased to exist. The Bodhisattva no longer had this feeling. The suttas refer to this state as "seclusion from elation"[*], "abandonment of elation"[†] or "seclusion from the sensual pleasure of elation".[‡]

2. **Abiding in Equanimity**: at the same time, the Bodhisattva experienced serenity, equanimity and tranquility when his mind came into contact with objects. His emotional mind no longer has the environment where it can arise. Even when the six objects of the senses[13] appeared before the six sense-organs[14], they could not activate the six consciousnesses. This is called the state of "**Equanimity**". The Bodhisattva continued to dwell in this state of serenity and calmness, which is referenced in the suttas as "abiding in equanimity". Equanimity here refers to a state of "**awake awareness**" of the surrounding environment while the chattering mind remains silent. This is the main outcome of the third stage of meditation. In Zen Buddhist terminology, one's

---

[*] Samyutta Nikāya, "The Connected Discourses of the Buddha", SN 54:1 "One Thing", Aṅguttara Nikāya, "The Numerical Discourses of the Buddha", Book of Nines, AN 9:41 "Tapussa"
[†] Dīrgha Āgama, DĀ 20, "Ambattha" sutra
[‡] Madhyama Āgama, MĀ 44, "Discourse on Awareness" sutra

CHAPTER 3: THE DECISIVE STAGE

true nature is present; in Early Buddhist terminology, the **Suchness-mind** is present; in modern neuroscience terminology, there is **self-cognitive awareness**. What only remains then is a silent cognitive awareness of the state of "no-talk".

Once a stable state of Equanimity is attained, the meditator will experience a state of wordless awake awareness in which the mind is serene, unperturbed, and un-attached to objects when the six sense-organs come into contact with the six objects of senses. However, if the state of equanimity is not stable, one remains attached to objects, and inner talk and inner dialogue will arise.

3. **Full and clear awareness**: after abiding in the state of Equanimity for a short while, the Bodhisattva recognized that his mind was continuously in the state of being clearly aware of the surrounding environment as well as any feelings that arose in his body without being perturbed. This is because, at that moment, his mind faculty, intellect, consciousness and egotistical self were all inactive, and therefore he had a very clear awareness without any *inner talk, inner dialogue* or *thought formation* coming into play. What remained was only a silent and awake awareness of the surrounding environment. This state is referred to in the suttas as "full and clear awareness". This is awareness by ultimate cognition, and not by the awakening consciousness because the awakening consciousness comes from the dualistic mind, in which the speech formation process keeps being triggered to describe the characteristics of this awareness by the consciousness.

4. **Equanimous awareness and dwelling in bliss**: at that moment, the Bodhisattva's body and mind reached a state of balance and harmony. As the Perception aggregate was silent, so were the Mental Formations and Consciousness aggregates. The egotistical self was absent. The Bodhisattva was in a state of equanimity and full awareness, which corresponds to the state of **silent awareness of the no-talk state**. This state is referred to in the suttas as "equanimous awareness". ("Equanimity" here refers to calmness, detachment and serenity, while awareness refers to the wordless or "right" awareness in which there is no inner talk and inner dialogue. As soon as inner talk and inner dialogue arise, the mind immediately falls into dualism.) As his body and mind were in balance, the Bodhisattva experienced a sense of bliss enveloping his entire body. The suttas referred to this state as "his body perceived a pleasant feeling". In order to maintain this state of bliss, the Bodhisattva continued to maintain his equanimous awareness. The Buddha later categorized this state as the third stage of meditation. He said that the Holy Ones, meaning enlightened beings, call this state *"equanimous and aware, dwelling in bliss, realizing and abiding in the third stage of meditation"*.

5. **An illness**: however, a short while later, the Bodhisattva recognized that to continue to abide in this state of bliss would become an "illness". This is because the sense of bliss continued to appear in his mind and that caused his mind to pay attention to it[*]. He realized that if he maintained the sense of bliss, his mind would continue to have an object to abide in and he would not be able to

---

[*] Aṅguttara Nikāya, "The Numerical Discourses of the Buddha", Book of Nines, AN 9:41 "Tapussa".

reach a higher level. For this reason, he decided to immerse deeper in equanimity so that no feeling phenomena could affect his mind. He would then be able to attain a state of samādhi without any feeling, sensation or perception.

The Bodhisattva eventually attained a stable state of equanimity. Although his mind abided in the sense of bliss ("abiding in bliss"), the feeling of bliss could not influence his mind. The Buddha said:

But such pleasant feeling that arose and remain in me did not influence my mind.

Summary

1. While the state of "samādhi without inner talk and inner dialogue" of the second stage of meditation is characterized by the **immobility of the speech formation process**, the highest level of the third stage of meditation is characterized by the **immobility of the thought formation process**, where the Feelings and Sensations aggregate and the Perception aggregate become silent. The meditator experiences a mind that is equanimous, detached and serene, one that is acutely aware but is not attached to any objects. This is called the state of "equanimity". This is a state of samādhi where the mind is not attached to feelings, sensations and perceptions. Mental factors[15] are absent as inner talk and inner dialogue are both silent. Behind these three processes is the state of "awake awareness".

This state is also called in the suttas "full and clear awareness". Buddhist Commentary Masters categorized it as "clear awareness samādhi" (*sampajañña-samādhi*) or "peaceful and tranquil samādhi" (*appanā-samādhi*).

2. To attain a stable state of equanimity, the meditator must go through one of two steps: (a) Gain control of the **thought formation process**[16] (which includes the Feelings and Sensations aggregate and the Perception aggregate) or (b) Attain **awake awareness** while sitting in meditation.

Realizing and abiding in the fourth stage of meditation

Brief recapitulation: after attaining the third stage of meditation in a stable manner, the Bodhisattva continued to abide in the state of bliss. He perceived more and more acutely the sense of bliss that enveloped his entire body and mind... He enjoyed this feeling, however he realized that if he maintained this state of enjoyment, this would become a "suffering"[*].

He then continued to immerse himself deeper in Equanimity or full-and-clear-awareness, so that his mind did not get attached to the feeling of *bliss*, even though this state of bliss was still in existence.

Eventually, he attained the state of samādhi in which there is no feeling or sensation.

Entering the fourth stage of meditation: as he went deeper into samādhi with the state of equanimity, his

---

[*] At times, the Buddha also called the clinging to the attainment of each stage of meditation as "suffering" or "illness" because the clinging would prevent us from progressing to a higher stage of meditation. In this instance, "suffering" carries the same meaning as "illness". In the Aṅguttara Nikāya, "The Numerical Discourses of the Buddha", AN 9:34 "Nibbāna", Venerable Sāriputta explained thus: "If while that bhikkhu is dwelling in this way, perception and attention accompanied by the pleasure connected with equanimity occur in him, he feels it as an affliction. Just as pain might arise for one feeling pleasure only to afflict him ... But the Blessed One has called affliction suffering..."

CHAPTER 3: THE DECISIVE STAGE 143

thought formation process became immobile: concepts and thinking no longer arose, no traces of feelings and sensations or perception could perturb his mind. At that time, the mind faculty, intellect, consciousness and the egotistical self completely disappeared, thoughts no longer arose, and mental factors became completely still. The state of **wordless awake awareness** progressively became **wordless cognitive awareness**. The Bodhisattva's mind fell into a state of immobility, and attachment to the feeling of bliss that was created by the state of equanimity gradually disappeared. At this point, "bliss and suffering" had been abandoned. The suttas call this "equanimous with bliss, equanimous with suffering", or "severing bliss, severing suffering"[*], or "extinguishing bliss, extinguishing suffering"[†] or "leaving elation and bliss"[‡].

Note: in this instance, "equanimity" means "letting go", whereas "suffering" means "illness". This illness is the enjoyment of the state of bliss, then dwelling in it, and then refusing to progress to the fourth stage of meditation. It is not suffering in the usual worldly sense of the word. Therefore, "equanimous with bliss, equanimous with suffering" means "letting go of bliss", and "letting go of the attachment to bliss".

(Letting go of elation is equivalent to "silent awareness".)

---

[*] In the words of the Samyutta Nikāya, SN 54:8: "May I, with the severing of comfort and pain, and with the passing away of previous elation and grief, enter and dwell in the fourth meditation..."
[†] In the words of the Madhyama Āgama, MĀ 44, "Discourse on Awareness" sutra: "The bhikkhu, with the extinguishing of bliss and suffering, and the extinguishing of previous elation and grief..."
[‡] In the words of the Dīrgha Āgama, DĀ 20, "Ambattha" sutra: "The bhikkhu, with the seclusion from elation and bliss, and with the extinguishing of previous feelings and sensations of elation and grief..."

(Abiding in equanimity is equivalent to the two words "No Talk".)

Results: at this point, previous feelings and sensations of joy and sadness (or elation and grief) no longer have the environment to arise. This is mentioned in the suttas as "the extinguishing of previous feelings and sensations of elation and grief…".

The Bodhisattva's mind was in a deep state of tranquility. His consciousness was immobile. The energy of his *wordless cognitive awareness* gained strength and he fell deeply into a state of samādhi with no object. His breath would automatically pause intermittently (this phenomenon is also called "pure breathing"). This is similar to holding the breath. His body would by itself occasionally take in a deep breath, then stop, and then repeat this pattern. This situation occurred during his entire meditation session.

At this point, the Bodhisattva's mind was no longer affected by the feeling of bliss, although this pleasant feeling was present in his entire body. This state is called in the suttas "no bliss, no suffering". At the same time, there was only a pure awareness that was generated by his equanimous mind (which is the state of "equanimity"). This state is called in the suttas "pure and equanimous awareness". In this state the dualistic awareness of the subject knowing the object was completely absent. The only thing remaining was a **stable stream of wordless cognitive awareness**.

The Buddha recounted this state to Aggivessana thus:

Now, Aggivessana, with the abandoning of bliss and suffering, as with the earlier disappearance of elation and grief, I entered upon and abided in the fourth meditation: purity of equanimity and awareness, neither bliss nor

CHAPTER 3: THE DECISIVE STAGE 145

suffering. But such pleasant feeling that arose and remain in me did not influence my mind. (MN 36:37)

Following this state, the Bodhisattva fell deeply into a state of samādhi where the **three mental formations were completely immobile**: speech formation, thought formation and bodily formation[17]. The egotistical self was completely absent. He maintained this state of immobility of mind over several days, following which supernatural energies started to emerge in his clear and pure mind. He had truly achieved enlightenment and self-liberation.

Understanding the value of the fourth stage of meditation

We can draw two important lessons from the Bodhisattva's success in the fourth stage of meditation:

1. Key element of the fourth stage of meditation: Whereas the main characteristic of the third stage of meditation is the non-attachment to the objects of feelings and sensations, also called Equanimity, the fourth level is characterized by the Immobility of mind or the presence of the "*tathā*-mind".

   The main characteristics of the *tathā*-mind are:

   - The mind faculty, consciousness, intellect and egotistical self are all absent.

   - Mental factors are completely still.

   - The three mental formations: speech formation, thought formation and bodily formation are completely silent.

   - Behind this silence is a stable flow of wordless cognitive awareness that has truly emerged.

2. How can one attain the fourth stage of meditation? There are three ways:

First method: systematically practicing the three levels of wordless awareness in order to gain control of the mental murmur (*manojalpa*) in a stable manner.

- Experience Silent Awareness and Awake awareness.
- Experience Wordless Cognitive Awareness.

The focus of these three processes is to isolate the networks that constitute the Perception aggregate, leading to the immobilization of the speech formation and thought formation processes. The Perception aggregate plays a central role in this process. If it is immobile, the "naming" and "conceptualization" energies are absent and the mind is as clear as a cloudless blue sky.

Second method: not exercising effort. This occurs when the meditator enters samādhi at will, "at the snap of the fingers". If effort is involved in the practice, the egotistical self and phenomena will be present. Feelings and sensations, perceptions, the mind faculty, consciousness, intellect, egotistical self and mental factors will immediately be present. Tension will result and relaxation will vanish. As a result dualistic thought will be present. These are the signs of a perturbed mind. If this is the case, one cannot attain the fourth stage of meditation. To achieve effortlessness, one must first practice regularly and continuously in order to achieve the requisite elements of the first three stages of meditation. Just like the Bodhisattva who attained the fourth stage of meditation only after a long period of strenuous practice. It was only then that he managed to vanquish both egotistical self and phenomena by controlling the speech formation and thought formation processes. Once he entered the fourth stage of meditation, he was in a state of complete relaxation.

Third method: attaining the *Tathā*-mind. This occurs when the meditator has attained the states of *silent awareness* and *awake awareness* in a completely stable manner. All conceptual thinking and discursive reasoning have been "cleansed". The mind becomes empty. Feelings, sensations and perceptions cannot affect the consciousness and mind-consciousness. Mental factors are still. The egotistical self and phenomena are absent. Evidently, the dualistic mind cannot be present.

Underneath this state is the wordless cognitive awareness that has clearly emerged. This is a mind that is totally pure, without any marks or blemishes. It is the stable foundation of Signless Samādhi, or Suchness Samādhi.

Summary

1. **Value of the fourth stage of meditation**: while in sitting meditation, the meditator attains an immobile mind or Suchness-mind. We can compare this state of immobile mind to the Right Samādhi state of the Noble Eightfold Path and the Signless Samādhi state of the Three Gates to Liberation.

2. **Effect**: the effect of the fourth stage of meditation is the complete elimination of mental defilements. The mind is liberated, knowledge is liberated. Sorrow and suffering cease. The body and mind are balanced and transformed. Spiritual insights blossom and spiritual

wisdom develops further. The potential for enlightenment gradually emerges from the cognitive awareness faculty.

3. **Necessary conditions**: although samādhi is developed by practicing in the four postures, in the fourth stage of meditation the emphasis is on the sitting posture rather than the walking, standing or lying postures. It is only through a stable sitting position that biological effects occur in the body, mind, spiritual wisdom and especially the brain of the meditator. First come the elimination of mental defilements, then balance of body and mind and blossoming of spiritual wisdom. Furthermore, at this stage, we are no longer fighting wandering thoughts but are really in the process of developing the potential of our Buddha-nature. At this stage, wandering thoughts have been totally vanquished and we are abiding in the *tathā*-mind. Without being in a sitting posture, we cannot develop the potential for enlightenment that is innate in our self-cognitive awareness faculty.

Meditators who have not experienced samādhi or do not appreciate the value of samādhi in attaining body and mind balance and spiritual wisdom development may overlook the value of the sitting meditation posture. Like Zen Master Nanyue Huairang who criticized Mazu Daoyi[18] for wanting to "polish a rock into a mirror", they may criticize those who practice sitting meditation and consider it an "illness".

4. **Essence of the fourth stage**: although the *Suchness-mind*, or *immobile mind*, and Signless Samādhi are highlighted in the fourth stage of meditation, in reality the essence of the fourth stage is built upon the

foundation of *silent awareness*. This is the state of clear awareness without any trace of thought or verbal chattering in it. The Suchness-mind, the immobile mind, Suchness Samādhi and Signless Samādhi are built on the foundation of stable silent awareness. In this state, inner talk and inner dialogue no longer arise. If one wishes to enter the fourth stage of meditation but fails to control the speech formation process while sitting in meditation, one's thought formation process will be activated.

For this reason, the necessary condition for entering the fourth stage of meditation is attaining a state of completely *stable silent awareness*. If we fail to attain a completely stable silent awareness state while in sitting meditation, the consciousness and egotistical self will find an opportunity to arise. The speech formation process will then insert itself and occasionally arise. Our mind will become perturbed, both egotistical self and phenomena will appear and our sitting meditation session will become an inner battleground involving inner talk and inner dialogue on many topics.

2

SPIRITUAL REALIZATION

The light of enlightenment started to appear

For the first time after six years of hard practice, the Bodhisattva sat in meditation with his body and mind totally relaxed. Effort, willpower and thought about practice methods were no longer present in his mind. His body and mind fell into a state of immobility. He sat with his body still like a statue and it appeared as though his breath had stopped. His mind was completely pure and in clear awareness, and did not pursue anything that happened in the surrounding environment. Although his perceptual patterns were still active in his body, they did not affect his mind because the speech formation and thought formation processes were completely still. At the same time the energy of his cognitive awareness – which is the energy of the unborn knowledge – became more and more stable and expansive.

Time passed by slowly and space seemed motionless. The Bodhisattva continued to be immersed deep in the state of immobile samādhi.

In the last night of the fourth week, while in the state of samādhi with immobile mind at the fourth stage of meditation, three supernatural energies, also called the "Three Insights"[19], gradually appeared clearly in the Bodhisattva's mind, in the same way as objects reflect on a clear and spotless mirror. The light of enlightenment started to shine in the Bodhisattva's pure mind.

CHAPTER 3: THE DECISIVE STAGE

The elucidation power of the *tathā*-mind or Buddha-nature gradually threw light on all the unsolvable issues that had eluded the Bodhisattva. The elucidation was very insightful and complete. The Bodhisattva clearly saw each event unfold as if they were right before his eyes. This was the energy of spiritual wisdom that had started to emerge.

Without haste, joy, questioning, fear or thinking, the Bodhisattva sat calmly in his state of immobile samādhi and silently looked at the events that progressively appeared in his mind. They kept appearing and the Bodhisattva kept silently looking at them in a state of immobile mind.

The answers to the intractable questions that had troubled his mind for many years now gradually appeared very clearly in his mind. In particular, the energy of the Third Insight elucidated the most important questions which, six years before, the Bodhisattva was so determined to find answers to, but without success. Now, he only needed to sit in a state of deep tranquility of mind – without exercising any effort, willpower, striving, aspiration, wishing, thinking, or other methods – to see the clear and complete answers to the most difficult problems. They appeared as-they-are. The Bodhisattva saw them as-they-are.

The Bodhisattva had his full spiritual realization. He saw the most original causes of birth, aging, sickness, death and human suffering. He knew where birth, aging, sickness, death and suffering came from and how to terminate them. This was the wonder of the unborn knowledge. The answers to his questions kept appearing clearly in his mind. Full spiritual realization (*abhisamaya*) is based on these principles.

It was so subtle! So wonderful! So deep and secret! So beyond reasoning! In no way did it accord with the perspective of those who had not experienced enlightenment.

He had his full spiritual realization. The light of enlightenment and liberation started to appear.

Inner spiritual realization turned into reality

1. Realizing the Insight into Own Past Lives

First, in the first watch[20] of the night (approximately from 7pm to 10pm), the Bodhisattva realized the intuitive wisdom called "Insight into Own Past Lives", remembering all of his own past lives, from one past life to innumerable past lives.

2. Realizing the Insight into the Divine Vision

In the second watch of the night (approximately from 10pm to 1am), the Bodhisattva realized the Insight into the Divine Vision, seeing very clearly all living beings dying from one life and being reborn into another life.

3. Realizing the Insight into the Termination of Mental Defilements

Finally, in the third and last watch of the night (approximately from 1am to 4am), the Bodhisattva realized the Insight into the Termination of Mental Defilements. This was an insight into the true nature of suffering and mental defilements, and the path that led to the termination of suffering and mental defilements. He knew as-they-are suffering, the causes for suffering and the path that leads to the end of suffering for all human beings. He saw clearly the nature of mental defilements, the causes of mental defilements and the path that leads to the end of mental defilements for all human beings. At this point, his mind was free from the various categories of mental defilements, caused by desires[21], craving for existence[22] and ignorance[23]. He clearly had a cognitive knowledge of: *"I am liberated. Birth is destroyed. The holy life has been lived. What had to be done has been done. There is no more coming into any state of being"* (Majjhima Nikāya, MN 36:43).

At that moment, dawn started to break. The Bodhisattva had truly attained his spiritual realization. The Born, which consists of the consciousness, mind faculty and intellect, was eliminated. The Unborn became permanently present.

The history of spirituality has recorded the Bodhisattva's exceptional spiritual realization. He was a person who, for a long time and with a strong determination, had struggled against the desires and craving of the egotistical self and against demons that arose from the worldly mind; sought enlightenment and liberation; but could not find the way. Now that his mind was completely still and empty, devoid of thinking, will, effort, aims and aspiration, he entered samādhi over many days and suddenly all the questions that had eluded his comprehension for so long were elucidated in a wonderful manner in his own mind. He had a full spiritual realization. This was truly an exceptional event in the world.

However, this exceptional event was not an accident, but was built upon the foundation of a stable samādhi state. Before that point, the Bodhisattva had gone through three stages of samādhi. In the fourth stage, his mind had progressed deep into the process of "no thought over a long and sustained period". Over many days, his mind was in a state of complete purity. His intellect was inactive. His consciousness was still. His thinking was silenced. His egotistical self was absent. He was not asleep, he had not lost consciousness, his mind had not left his body, and he was not haggard like someone under hypnotism. He had complete **awake awareness** and clear **cognitive awareness** of everything that happened inside his body and in the external environment. It was on this basis that he attained his full spiritual realization.

Full spiritual realization is always based on **wordless cognitive awareness**. It is about something that we did not know previously, but now know very clearly and completely. It is something that we did not intend to attain, but now have attained.

The development of spiritual wisdom, enlightenment and inner spiritual realization all happen on this basis. Enlightenment is not based on developing the intellect or consciousness, but on expanding the potential for enlightenment inside our self-cognitive awareness nature, or our ***tathā*-mind**. The Buddha described this state of mind as "beyond reasoning" (*atakkāvacara*). This is an important point that we need to note. If we hold onto the consciousness, the mind faculty and the intellect, we will never attain spiritual realization, will not be able to develop our spiritual wisdom, and will not be able to free our knowledge and our mind.

The process of spiritual realization

To help Aggivessana understand clearly the process of spiritual realization, the Buddha described to him the principles underlying his realization of the Three Insights. First he recounted his realization of the Insight into his Own Past Lives:

When my mind was thus in a state of bare cognition[24], purified, bright, unblemished[25], rid of imperfection, malleable²⁶, wieldy, steady, and imperturbable, I directed it to knowledge of my own past lives. I recollected my manifold past lives, that is, one birth, two births, three births, four births, five births, ten births, twenty births, thirty births, forty births, fifty births, a hundred births, a thousand births, a hundred thousand births, many eons of world-destruction²⁷, many eons of world-formation²⁸, many eons of world-destruction and formation: 'There I was so named, of such a clan, with such an appearance, such was my nutriment, such my experience of pleasure and pain, such my life-term; and passing away from there, I reappeared elsewhere; and there too I was so named, of such a clan, with such an appearance, such was my nutriment, such my experience of pleasure and pain, such my life-term; and passing away from there, I reappeared here'. Thus with their aspects and particulars I recollected my manifold past lives. This was the first true knowledge attained by me in the first watch of the night... (MN 36:38)

Then he described the process of his realization of the Insight into the Divine Vision. This was how he clearly saw the results of people's rebirth into different families, clans, societies and social classes; how they differ in their experience of wealth, happiness, poverty, and misery; how they have bodies with different appearance and shape. He saw that all these events were caused by the three forms of karma – speech, intention and action karma – either virtuous or evil karma, right or wrong karma, which they have generated in their past life. He said:

When my mind was thus in a state of bare cognition, purified, bright, unblemished, rid of imperfection, malleable, wieldy, steady, and imperturbable, I directed it to knowledge of the passing away and reappearance of beings. Thus with the divine vision, which is purified and surpasses the human, I saw beings passing away and reappearing, inferior[29] and superior[30], fair and ugly, fortunate and unfortunate, and I understood how beings pass on according to their actions. Those beings who were endowed with bad conduct of body, speech, and mind, who reviled the holy ones, held wrong views and undertook actions under the influence of wrong views, with the break-up of the body, after death, reappeared in the plane of deprivation, a bad destination, the lower realms, in hell. But those beings who were endowed with good conduct of body, speech and mind, who did not revile the holy ones, who held right views and undertook actions under the influence of right views, with the break-up of the body, after death, reappeared in good destinations, in the heavenly world. Thus, by means of the divine vision, purified and surpassing the human, I saw beings passing away and reappearing, and I discerned how they are inferior and superior, fair and ugly, fortunate and unfortunate in accordance with their actions. This was the second true knowledge attained by me in the second watch of the night ... (MN 36:40)

From his insights into the recollection of his own hundreds and thousands of past lives and the vision of the destruction and formation of worldly phenomena, the Buddha later established in his teaching the principle of how past lives and the law of karma affect all beings. This was the Doctrine of Dependent Origination, which brought together the three characteristics of worldly phenomena – Impermanence, Suffering and No-Self – and the law of cause and effect. He thus implicitly repudiated the belief of many past and contemporary religions at the time that a God created the world and all beings.

CHAPTER 3: THE DECISIVE STAGE

He would later use his Insight into the Divine Vision to enunciate in his teaching the law of causal conditions or law of cause and effect that applies to all beings. He clearly explained the causal conditions that led to the presence of beings in the human and heavenly realms. He repudiated the power of a God who decided the punishment or reward, good or bad fortune of human beings, as was the belief of traditional religions at the time. He considered that humans are masters of their own fate, and that there is no superior deity who decides their fate. People's fate is determined by their speech karma, intention karma and action karma that all depend on many causal conditions. Therefore people have the ability to change their fate by transforming the causal conditions that created their karma.

The Buddha subsequently recounted his realization of the Insight into the Termination of Mental Defilements in the third and last watch of the night. He described how he knew suffering and mental defilements as-they-are, the origins of suffering and mental defilements as-they-are, and the path to terminate suffering and mental defilements as-it-is. He said:

When my mind was thus in a state of bare cognition, purified, bright, unblemished, rid of imperfection, malleable, wieldy, steady, and imperturbable, I directed it to knowledge of the termination of defilements. I directly knew it as it actually is: 'This is suffering'; 'This is the origin of suffering'. 'This is the cessation of suffering'; 'This is the way leading to the cessation of suffering'; 'These are the defilements'; 'This is the origin of the defilements'; 'This is the cessation of the defilements'; 'This is the way leading to the cessation of the defilements.'
(MN 36:42)

Based on his realization of the Insight into the Termination of Mental Defilements and the principle of seeing and knowing suffering and mental defilements *as-they-are*, the Buddha later praised, in his teaching, seeing and knowing things as-they-are as true knowledge and called the knowing by reasoning as false knowledge. He also taught how to attain as-it-is seeing and knowing by using the awareness faculty when observing objects and worldly phenomena.

Based on his Insight into the Termination of Mental Defilements, he also established the Four Noble Truths in which he described the types of suffering, the origins of suffering, the cessation of suffering and the path leading to the cessation of suffering which is the Noble Eightfold Path. He explained the practice of the Noble Eightfold Path in detail. He explained that mental defilements are the cause that generates karma. Human beings are the victims of their own mental defilements. Mental defilements can be eliminated through samādhi and spiritual paññā wisdom.

The final accomplishment

Finally, the Buddha declared that from his realization of the Insight into the Termination of Mental Defilements, he was liberated from mental defilements and was totally liberated so that he would not be reborn in any realms of the world. He said:

When I knew and saw thus, my mind was liberated from the defilement of sensual desire, from the defilement of existence, and from the defilement of ignorance. When it was liberated there came the knowledge: 'It is liberated.' I directly knew: 'Birth is destroyed, the holy life has been lived, what had to be done has been done, there is no more coming to any state of being'. This was the third true knowledge attained by me in the third watch of the night. (MN 36:43)

Through his realization of the termination of all types of mental defilements, the Buddha indicated later in his teachings that mental defilements are the cause of the endless cycle of birth, death and rebirth. One must practice samādhi meditation to eliminate mental defilements. He established the three meditation methods of Precepts (*Sīla*), Stillness of mind (*Samādhi*), and Wisdom (*Paññā*), and the four practice methods that span from beginner to advanced levels: Contemplation (*Anupassanā*), Tranquility (*Samatha*), Stillness of Mind (*Samādhi*) and Wisdom (*Paññā*).

With regard to samādhi meditation, he emphasized the "unified mind" or "inner serenity and unified mind" (*cetaso-ekodhibhāva*). This is the necessary state on which the state of samādhi without inner talk and inner dialogue is built. It is also the foundation of the Right Samādhi in the Noble Eightfold Path.

He praised Signless Samādhi as the ultimate vehicle that leads to ultimate enlightenment and liberation that he had attained. He rejected the four levels of Yoga meditation which are: the Base of Boundless Space, the Base of Boundless Consciousness, the Base of Nothingness and the Base of Neither Perception nor Non-Perception (Khuddaka Nikāya, "The Minor Collection of the Discourses of the Buddha", Udāna "Exclamations", Ud80).

Vow became reality

After leaving home at the age of 29 and six years of sustained struggle against his own mind, Prince Siddhattha Gotama finally sat in meditation under the *pipphala* tree and vanquished his egotistical self and the army of inner demons of his mind by progressing through the four stages of his own meditation technique. He completely *abandoned* all that was born, consisting of the reasoning intellect, the calculating mind faculty and discriminating consciousness.

As a result, he attained the Unborn and was liberated from birth, aging, sickness and death along with sorrow and defilements.

In the Ariyapariyesanā Sutta, "The Noble Search", the Buddha described to his disciples how he attained the Unborn:

Then, Bhikkhus, being myself subject to birth, having understood the danger in what is subject to birth, seeking the unborn supreme security from bondage, Nibbāna, I attained the unborn supreme security from bondage, Nibbāna; being myself subject to aging, having understood the danger in what is subject to aging, seeking the non-aging supreme security from bondage, Nibbāna, I attained the non-aging supreme security from bondage, Nibbāna; being myself subject to sickness, having understood the danger in what is subject to sickness, seeking the unailing supreme security from bondage, Nibbāna, I attained the unailing supreme security from bondage, Nibbāna; being myself subject to death, having understood the danger in what is subject to death, seeking the deathless supreme security from bondage, Nibbāna, I attained the deathless supreme security from bondage, Nibbāna; being myself subject to sorrow, having understood the danger in what is subject to sorrow, seeking the sorrowless supreme security from bondage, Nibbāna, I attained the sorrowless supreme security from bondage, Nibbāna; being myself subject to defilement, having understood the danger in what is subject to defilement, seeking the undefiled supreme security from bondage, Nibbāna, I attained the undefiled supreme security from bondage, Nibbāna. The knowledge and vision arose in me: 'My deliverance is unshakeable; this is my last birth; now there is no renewal of being.' (Majjhima Nikāya, "The Middle Length Discourses of the Buddha", Ariyapariyesanā Sutta "The Noble Search", MN 26:18).

After six years of hardship, Prince Siddhattha Gotama's vow finally became reality. He had attained enlightenment and the **Unborn**. He was 35 years of age.

The *pipphala* tree under which he sat in meditation was later called the Bodhi tree, meaning the tree of enlightenment. The place where he attained enlightenment became known as Bodh Gaya, or enlightenment place (*bodhimaṇḍa*).

From that time, the history of his enlightenment would forever enter into the spiritual consciousness of all those who seek enlightenment and self-liberation. His model of enlightenment and liberation through self-reliant practice has developed deep roots in the spirituality of Eastern nations, especially for those who travel along the path of samādhi meditation. This model of enlightenment and liberation is based on the **immobile mind**, or the ***tathā-mind***. This was the meditation stage that led to the enlightenment of the Buddha.

REFERENCES
FOR CHAPTER III

SUTTAS

1. Kinh Tăng Chi Bộ (Aṅguttara Nikāya) – Translated into Vietnamese by Hòa Thượng Thích Minh Châu, Saigon, 1996, Book 4, "Book of the Nines", Sutta #31 "Progressive Cessation" pp. 152-153, Sutta #33 "Dwellings" pp. 154-155, Sutta #41 "Tapussa" pp. 197-203

2. Kinh Trung Bộ (Majjhima Nikāya) – Translated into Vietnamese by Hòa Thượng Thích Minh Châu, Saigon, 1986, Book 1, Sutta #4 "Fear and Dread" pp. 53-57, Sutta # 26 "The Noble Search" pp. 373-378, Sutta # 36 "The Greater Discourse to Saccaka" pp. 541-544

3. Kinh Trường A Hàm 1 (Dīrghāgama), DĀ 44 "Awareness" Sutra, p. 611

4. Kinh Trường A Hàm 2 (Dīrghāgama), DĀ 20 "Ambattha" Sutra, pp. 35-41

5. Kinh Trung A Hàm 1 (Madhyamāgama), MĀ 2 "The Day of Liberation Tree" Sutra, pp. 21-22

6. Kinh Tương Ưng Bộ (Samyutta Nikāya) – Translated into Vietnamese by Hòa Thượng Thích Minh Châu, Saigon, 1993, Part 5, "Right Awareness" Sutta pp. 220-221, "The Lamp" Sutta pp. 472-475

7. Kinh Tiểu Bộ (Khuddaka Nikāya) – Translated into Vietnamese by Hòa Thượng Thích Minh Châu, Saigon, 1999, Udāna Ud 1.10 (Ud 6) ("Bāhiya" Sutta) pp. 126-

CHAPTER 3: THE DECISIVE STAGE 163

130, Udāna Ud 8.1 (Ud 80) ("Nibbāna" Sutta) pp. 265-267

8. The Numerical Discourses of the Buddha – A Translation of the Aṅguttara Nikāya – Translated by Bhikkhu Bodhi, Wisdom Publications, Boston, 2012. "Book of the Nines", Sutta #31 "Progressive Cessation" pp. 152-153, Sutta #33 "Dwellings" pp. 154-155, Sutta #41 "Tapussa" pp. 197-203

9. The Middle Length Discourses of the Buddha – A New Translation of the Majjhima Nikāya – Translated by Bhikkhu Ñāṇamoli and Bhikkhu Bodhi, Wisdom Publications, Boston, 1995. Sutta # 26 "The Noble Search", Sutta # 36 "The Greater Discourse to Saccaka"

10. Handful of Leaves – Volume 2 – An Anthology from the Majjhima Nikāya – Translated by Thānissaro Bhikkhu (Geoffrey DeGraff), Printed by Metta Forest Monastery – 2014, Sutta # 26 "The Noble Search", Sutta # 36 "The Greater Discourse to Saccaka"

COMMENTARIES

11. The Buddha and His Teachings, by Mahāthera Nārada, pp. 18, 27, 34-35; 18-19.

12. The Buddha and His Dhamma, by Dr. B.R. Ambedkar, Taiwan, 1997, pp. 68-69; 73-75; 111-114, 119.

13. Buddhist Meditation in Theory and Practice, by Paravahera Vajirañāna Mahāthera, pp. 8-12, 37-43.

14. Before He Was Buddha, The Life of Siddhartha, by Hammalawa Saddhatissa, pp. 33-35.

15. Encyclopedia of Buddhism, Ed. G.P. Malasasekera, O.B.E. Vol. I, pp. 105-107; Vol. II, pp. 97-102; Vol. III, pp. 178-180; 207; 249-251; 364-370; 490-500; Vol. IV, pp. 206-207; 312-318; 478-480.

16. The Life of Buddha, by A. Ferdinand Herold, Tokyo 1954, pp. 112-113.

17. The Living Thoughts of Gotama the Buddha, by Ananda K. Coomaraswamy and I. B. Horner, New Delhi, 1981, pp. 44-45.

18. A Survey of Buddhism, by Bhikkhu Aangharakshita, Colorado, 1980, pp. 151-153.

19. Buddhist Scriptures, by Edward Conze, 1959, pp. 49-51.

20. Buddhism, by K.S. Chen, Woodbury, New York, 1968, pp. 22-23.

21. Buddhism in Translations, Henry Clarke Warren, New Delhi, 1986, pp. 71-74; 83-87.

22. History of Theravāda Buddhism in South-East Asia, by Kanai Lal Hazra, New Delhi, 1996, pp. 12-13.

CHAPTER IV

THE ENLIGHTENMENT PROCESS

1

THE FOUNDATIONS OF THE BUDDHA'S ENLIGHTENMENT

Before we detail the Buddha's process of spiritual enlightenment, we need to understand the meaning of his enlightenment and how this historical event unfolded.

Historical event

Today at Bodh Gaya, there is a roofless house called the "Jewel House". According to legend, the history of the commemorative monuments at Bodh Gaya goes back to King Aśoka. After he renounced his brutal ways and converted to Buddhism, King Aśoka invited Upagupta, the fourth Buddhist Patriarch, to Pataliputtra to recount to him the events that marked the life of the Buddha. Following that, King Aśoka decided to erect shrines at the locations where the Buddha was born, where he grew up, practiced and attained enlightenment, where he set the wheel of *dhamma* into motion, and where he passed from this world, at Kusinagara. At Bodh Gaya, King Aśoka built monuments at seven places to commemorate the seven events that occurred over the seven weeks after the Buddha attained enlightenment. The first four weeks during which the Buddha sat down at the foot of the Bodhi tree to start his practice were not taken into account. For this reason, the event marking the Buddha's realization of the Law of Dependent Origination was attributed to the fourth week.

If we add the first four weeks during which the Buddha attained Immobility Samādhi to the four weeks recorded at Bodh Gaya, we can conclude that the Buddha attained enlightenment in the eighth week when he realized the Law of Dependent Origination and the Law of Dependently Arisen Phenomena.

In what follows, we use the format of hypothetical questions and answers to provide readers with a clear exposé of the topic.

Question: Master, could you please explain the meaning of the word "enlightenment" as it applies to the Buddha?

Answer: The word "enlightenment" is used here specifically for the Buddha. It means that the Buddha attained his objective of ultimate enlightenment. This is a state that only the Buddha has attained. The word "enlightenment" refers here to the state of Supreme Full Enlightenment and indicates that Gotama the Bodhisattva had become the historical Buddha.

Question: Master, could you please explain what "historical Buddha" means?

Answer: The words "historical Buddha" mean that the Buddha was a real person in the history of mankind. He is not the fruit of the fertile imagination of humans but is a real human who was born like every other human. He had a father and a mother, a birth place; he grew up preoccupied by a great concern that eventually led him to renounce everything that he had and search for spiritual teachers. Following several failures, including a near death experience when he was rescued by a young shepherdess who offered him a bowl of milk that resuscitated him, he finally found the practice that led to enlightenment. He had found the answer to the question that preoccupied him.

The most notable locations marking his spiritual journey include Bodh Gaya where he attained enlightenment; Bārānasi where he set the *dhamma* wheel into motion; Kusinagara where he passed from this world; Lumbīnī where he was born; and Kapilāvatthu where he grew up. These events are evidence that the Buddha was a *real* person. This is the significance of the words "historical Buddha".

Question: Master, why do you need to emphasize the point that he was the historical Buddha?

Answer: Around 300 years after the Buddha had passed from this world, several schools of Buddhism emerged. Some of these schools *invented* other Buddhas who did not exist in the history of humanity. I emphasize the importance of the historical Buddha to remind today's practitioners that they need to follow the path laid out by the historical Buddha if they wish to end suffering, attain enlightenment and be liberated from the cycle of birth and death.

Question: Master, what is the *path* laid out by the historical Buddha?

Answer: It is the path of samādhi meditation.

Question: Master, could you please explain which method the Buddha used to attain enlightenment?

Answer: The Buddha attained enlightenment in the eighth week after he sat down at the foot of the Bodhi tree, through a process of self-generated response, which means that he actually no longer applied any method. He dwelt in his *tathā*-mind, which is a state of *mind beyond words*, which the Buddha described as *"a mind in a state of bare cognition, pure, bright, unblemished, rid of imperfection,*

CHAPTER IV: THE ENLIGHTENMENT PROCESS   169

malleable, beyond reasoning, wieldy, steady, and imperturbable...". He then directed his mind toward the contemplation of worldly phenomena. At this point, his potential for enlightenment revealed to him the answers to the questions that preoccupied him, and he saw the four characteristics of worldly phenomena as well as their essential nature.

Question: Master, before we get into detail about the nature of the Buddha's enlightenment, could you please explain on which foundation this enlightenment was based?

Answer: Similarly to the situation at the end of the fourth week when the Buddha realized the Three Insights, in the eighth week the Buddha went back to dwelling in the state of Immobility Samādhi, that is in his *tathā*-mind.

Question: Master, could you please explain in broad terms what Immobility Samādhi is?

Answer: This is the state where the three mental formation processes are immobile. First, the speech formation process is immobile, which means that inner talk and inner dialogue are both silent; this is the outcome of the second stage of samādhi, called samādhi without inner talk and inner dialogue. Second, the thought formation process is immobile, which means that the Feelings and Sensations aggregate and the Perception aggregate are both still; this is the outcome of the third stage of samādhi, called Full and Clear Awareness samādhi. Third, the bodily formation process is immobile, which manifests through the breath stopping at intervals; this is also called "pure breathing".

Question: Master, could you please explain the meaning of *tathā*-mind?

Answer: *Tathā* means "as" or "as such". When combined with the word "mind", we get the "mind-as-such" or *tathā-mind*. It is the state of mind beyond words, which the Buddha called *atakkāvacara* (beyond the realm of reasoning).

Question: Master, is the state of Immobility Samādhi the same as the *tathā*-mind?

Answer: Exactly!

Question: Master, what other forms of samādhi is the state of Immobility Samādhi comparable to?

Answer: The state of Immobility Samādhi is also called Suchness Samādhi, or Signless Samādhi (which is one of the Three Gates to Liberation mentioned by the Buddha), or Non-abiding Samādhi (as mentioned in the Diamond Sutra), or Diamond Samādhi (as taught in Theravāda Buddhism). This is the highest level of samādhi in Buddhism.

2

THE ESSENCE OF

THE BUDDHA'S ENLIGHTENMENT

The suttas record that, after the Buddha realized the Three Insights, he remained in the area of the Bodhi tree for another seven weeks to further contemplate what he had just attained. During this period, he realized the **Law of Dependent Origination** and the **Law of Dependently Arisen Phenomena**, which are considered to be key elements of his enlightenment.

We will use the format of hypothetical questions and answers to clearly explain the process by which the Buddha attained enlightenment.

Question: Master, what other truths did the Buddha realize in the eighth week?

Answer: The Buddha realized the Law of Dependent Origination.

Question: Master, could you please tell us in what suttas is the Law of Dependent Origination recorded?

Answer: The Law of Dependent Origination is a very important teaching, and this is why the Buddha expounded it in many suttas compiled in the Nikāyas and Āgamas. The following are excerpts from a sutta in the Nikāyas:

And what, Bhikkhus, is dependent origination? With birth as a condition, aging-and-death comes to be. Whether there is an arising of Tathāgatas or no arising of Tathāgatas, that element still persists – the stableness of the Dhamma, the fixed course of the Dhamma, specific conditionality. A Tathāgata awakens to this and breaks through to it. Having done so, he explains it, teaches it, proclaims it, establishes it, discloses it, analyzes it, elucidates it. And he says: 'See! With birth as condition, Bhikkhus, comes aging-and-death'.

'With existence as condition, comes birth'... 'With clinging as a condition, comes existence'... 'With craving as condition, comes clinging'... 'With feelings and sensations as condition, comes craving'... 'With contact as condition, come feelings and sensations'... 'With the six sense bases as condition, comes contact' ... 'With name-and-form as condition, comes the six sense bases'... 'With consciousness as condition, comes name-and-form'... 'With mental formations as condition, comes consciousness'... 'With ignorance as condition, come mental formations'. Whether there is an arising of Tathāgatas or no arising of Tathāgatas, that element still persists – the stableness of the Dhamma, the fixed course of the Dhamma, specific conditionality. A Tathāgata awakens to this and breaks through to it. Having done so, he explains it, teaches it, proclaims it, establishes it, discloses it, analyzes it, elucidates it. And he says: 'See! With ignorance as condition, Bhikkhus, come mental formations'.

Thus, Bhikkhus, the Suchness in this, the indivisibleness, the identicalness, specific conditionality: this is called dependent origination. (Samyutta Nikāya, "The Connected Discourses of the Buddha", SN 12.20, "Conditions")

1. Four characteristics of the Law of Dependent Origination

Question: Master, what are the four characteristics of worldly phenomena?

CHAPTER IV: THE ENLIGHTENMENT PROCESS 173

Answer: When the Buddha contemplated worldly phenomena from his *tathā*-mind, he recognized the following:

- The absolute objectivity of worldly phenomena, called their Suchness (***Tathatā***) -nature

- This *Tathatā* cannot be divided, this is called their Indivisibleness (***Avitathatā***) -nature

- The *Tathatā* is the same for all worldly phenomena, this is called their Identicalness (***Anaññathatā***) -nature

- Each worldly phenomenon arises from the gathering of specific conditions; this is called their Specific Conditionality (***Idappaccayatā***) -nature.

Question: Master, could you please explain the meaning of *Tathatā*?

Answer: *Tathatā* means Suchness or in-that-way-ness.

Question: Master, could you please explain the meaning of *Avitathatā*?

Answer: With his Buddha's vision, the Buddha saw that the *Tathatā* is like a limitless emptiness that cannot be divided; this is called its Indivisibleness-nature.

Question: Master, could you please explain the meaning of *Anaññathatā*?

Answer: *Tathatā* is present in every worldly phenomenon and this *Tathatā* is the same, this is called its Identicalness-nature.

Question: And, Master, what is *Idappaccayatā*?

Answer: With his Buddha's vision, the Buddha saw that all things in the universe, from the largest like the sun to the smallest like a speck of dust, all are formed by the presence of specific conditions; this is called their Specific-Conditionality-nature.

Further explanations of the four characteristics of worldly phenomena

Question: Master, could you please provide further explanations of the four characteristics of worldly phenomena?

Answer: This is a fundamental aspect of the Buddha's enlightenment. While dwelling in his *tathā*-mind, the Buddha sat with his face turned toward the Nerañjarā River and saw through his Buddha's vision that all worldly phenomena have *Suchness*. This *Suchness* envelops the whole vast universe and cannot be divided. Every object, from the largest like the sun to the smallest like a speck of dust, all have *Suchness*. With his Buddha's vision, he also saw that worldly phenomena have their specific causal conditions; he called this characteristic Specific Conditionality (*Idappaccayatā*). This characteristic explains the differences in the phenomenal world.

Let me give you an example. The physical forms of objects such as mountains, rivers, earth, sand, water, plants, etc. have their own specific characteristics. Mountains are made of hard rocks, rivers have water, plants belong to many species; however inside and outside these objects there is Suchness. This Suchness cannot be divided; therefore the Suchness is the same for all objects. People are also formed by the presence of specific conditions, resulting in Asiatic, European, or African, etc. people.

Animals such as lions, tigers, panthers also have their own specific conditionality. Likewise, flowers and fruits have their own specific conditionality. Even the solar system has its own specific conditionality.

Specific conditionality is a universal principle that has always existed, regardless of whether the Buddha came into being or not. The Buddha called specific conditionality a *"fixed course of the dhamma"*. Under this principle, worldly phenomena are not created by a deity or a God. They evolve through a cycle of birth and death which is governed by the **law of cause and effect**. Underneath the law of cause and effect is the energy of the **law of change and transformation**. It is the law of change and transformation that causes changes in appearance, color, birth and death, etc. in the phenomenal world. The Buddha called the cycle of Arise-Remain-Decay-Cease-Transform a law that applies to "conditioned phenomena", which are phenomena that are formed by the presence of conditions. On the other hand, Suchness is not created by conditions, and this is why the Buddha called it an "unconditioned phenomenon".

The Buddha identified the four primordial characteristics of worldly phenomena as:

1. Suchness (*Tathatā*)
2. Indivisibleness (*Avitathatā*)
3. Identicalness (*Anaññathatā*)
4. Specific Conditionality (*Idappaccayatā*)

Question: Master, could you please explain further what Conditioned Phenomena are?

Answer: Conditioned Phenomena are things that are formed by the presence of many causes or many conditions. For this reason, Conditioned Phenomena are subject to the law of impermanence, the law of change and transformation, the law of cause and effect, while their essential nature is emptiness and illusory existence. All worldly phenomena, including human beings, are Conditioned Phenomena. The Buddha also used the term "The Born". The essential characteristics of worldly phenomena such as impermanence, change and transformation, no-self, specific conditionality, emptiness, illusion are generally called the Essential Nature of Phenomena (*Dhammatā*).

Question: And, Master, what are Unconditioned Phenomena?

Answer: Unconditioned Phenomena are things that are not created by conditions. Consequently, they do not change nor do they cease to exist. They are what the Buddha called "The Unborn". They are Suchness. In the Buddhist literature, they are also called the Essence of the Phenomenal World (*Dhammatā-dhātu*).

2. The formulation of the law of cause and effect

After contemplating the Law of Dependent Origination through the three watches of the night, the Buddha summarized it in the following four lines of verse:

This is, because that is.
This arises, because that arises.
This is not, because that is not.
This ceases, because that ceases.

These four lines of verse encapsulate the **Law of Cause and Effect**.

Question: Master, what is the Law of Cause and Effect?

CHAPTER IV: THE ENLIGHTENMENT PROCESS

Answer: It is a universal law that the Buddha discovered regarding the formation of the phenomenal world. This law does not involve the intervention of any deity. Phenomena are interdependent with each other; they do not exist in separation. Phenomena depend on each other for their creation, change, cessation and transformation into something else.

Each phenomenon arises due to a set of causes. The phenomenon is like a fruit (an effect) that comes from a seed (a cause), and in turn this "fruit" will be part of the conditions that create another "fruit", and so on. This is called the "endless cycle of dependent origination".

Question: Master, could you please provide an example?

Answer: This meditation class exists because there are many people who wish to learn about meditation. Thanks to this class many students will change their perspective on life; with this change in perspective their life will be in harmony; thanks to their harmonious life, their psychosomatic illnesses will be alleviated; thus their physical health will improve, they will experience peace and happiness, which will bring happiness to their family, etc.

Question: Master, according to the Law of Cause and Effect, can we find the original condition that starts the chain of causes and effects?

Answer: No. We cannot find the original condition since each phenomenon is formed by the presence of previous conditions. And no-one has the ability to find the original conditions.

Question: There are popular sayings such as "Each action brings commensurate consequence" or "Do good and you will encounter goodness, do bad and you will encounter badness." Master, could you please explain whether these sayings are in accordance with the Law of Cause and Effect?

Answer: These are subjective assertions which come from a worldly perspective and have a moral intent. By contrast, according to the Buddhist Law of Cause and Effect, if there is a cause then there must be an effect. The Buddha does not make a value judgment whether the cause or effect is good or bad since goodness or badness depends on the subjective view of each person. Therefore, the Law of Cause and Effect is an absolutely objective truth.

Question: Master, could you please explain to us the actual origin of the karma that affects us in this life?

Answer: According to the Buddhist Law of Cause and Effect, causes are generated either from this life or from previous lives. Both categories of causes push the individual to generate causal actions in the present moment.

Question: Master, could you please provide a concrete example?

Answer: For example, the Buddha saw in the chain of his own lives that previous lives were the causes of subsequent lives. He also saw that the condition of human beings in their present lives – whether they have good or bad character, whether they enjoy a long or short life, whether they are clever or dull, etc. – are entirely the consequences of their actions in previous lives.

3. The Law of Change and Transformation in the universe

Question: Master, could you please tell us what is the Law of Change and Transformation?

Answer: This law stipulates that worldly phenomena are subject to ceaseless change. The Buddha discovered this law when he attained enlightenment with the realization of the Law of Dependent Origination. The Law of Change and Transformation, when applied to the universe, is the cycle of "Arise-Remain-Decay-Cease-Transform". When applied to human beings it consists of the cycle of "Birth-Aging-Sickness-Death-Rebirth" and the "Twelve Links of Dependent Origination". Underneath these processes lies the energy of change and transformation.

Question: Master, what is the effect of the energy of change and transformation?

Answer: The effect is change in the form, color and quality of all worldly phenomena every second, every minute of time. From there, the Buddha discovered the Three Characteristics of Worldly Phenomena, which are: impermanence, suffering or conflict, and no-self or absence of real substance. The law of change and transformation results in the evolution, blossoming and change of worldly phenomena.

4. The essential characteristics of worldly phenomena

Question: Master, could you please tell us what the essential characteristics of worldly phenomena are?

Answer: They are:

- Equality,

- Change and transformation,
- Emptiness, and
- Illusion.

Explaining the essential characteristics of world phenomena

Question: Master, what is the Equality-nature?

Answer: Worldly phenomena consist of human beings, natural settings, objects, facts, events, etc. Every phenomenon has Suchness-nature or *Tathatā*, therefore they are considered to be equal.

Question: Master, could you please explain further what you just said. Human beings are worldly phenomena that consist of a material aspect and a spiritual aspect, also called "name and form". Which of these two aspects have the Equality-nature?

Answer: I would like to clarify the concept of worldly phenomena, called *dhammā* (in its plural form) in Pāli. This word has also been translated as "all things" or "all phenomena". Everything that comes into contact with the senses is considered worldly phenomena. Human beings consist of two parts. "Name", or the mind, is an important one; it manifests itself through states of mind which can be perceived by the senses, and is considered to be a worldly phenomenon. "Form", or the physical body, is the material part of human beings. Both name and form have Suchness-nature, and therefore are considered by the Buddha as having Equality-nature.

Question: Master, and what is the Change-and-Transformation-nature?

CHAPTER IV: THE ENLIGHTENMENT PROCESS

Answer: It is the ever-changing nature of worldly phenomena which change from one state to another state, from a form to another form, through the five stages of arise, remain, decay, cease and transform. The last stage, transform, leads to another cycle of arise, remain, decay, cease and transform, and so on. The Buddha called this process the "cycle of birth and death of worldly phenomena".

Question: Master, what is the Emptiness-nature?

Answer: Emptiness is the essential nature of worldly phenomena. It is the seed that creates the energy of change and transformation in the phenomenal world. Without their Emptiness-nature, worldly phenomena would not be able to change from one state to another.

Question: Master, does the sun also have Emptiness-nature?

Answer: As I have said, all worldly phenomena, from the largest ones such as the sun to the smallest ones such as a speck of dust, are formed from many causes and many conditions. This is why they continuously change as their underlying causes and conditions change. Their essential nature is Emptiness. Since the sun is a worldly phenomenon, it also has Emptiness-nature.

Question: Master, so the sun is also subject to the law of change and transformation?

Answer: Of course, the sun is subject to the law of change and transformation, which means that it also follows the cycle of arise, remain, decay, cease and transform.

Question: Master, and what is Illusion-nature?

Answer: Worldly phenomena exist when they come into contact with our senses; we think that they are real, but in reality they are not. Let me give you the example of a person's body. First, the person is born; s/he is given a name; then s/he grows up and becomes an adult; as time progresses, the person ages and dies. The Buddha called this process of change "illusion". The human body exists but it is not real as it changes continuously. Our emotions are another example. Our emotions change continuously, sometimes we feel love, at other times we feel sadness, longing, anger, etc.

5. **The essence of worldly phenomena**

Question: Master, what is the essence of worldly phenomena?

Answer: It is Suchness *(Tathatā)*.

Question: Master, could you please explain further about Suchness?

Answer: Suchness is the *true reality*. Nothing can be *added* to it nor *removed* from it. It simply is *as such*. Its essence is unchanging, immobile and ever-abiding. Nothing can be added to it nor removed from it, because it does not have the capacity to contain anything. It is beyond language. It is that which does not have a name. It simply means *as such is as such*. It is considered the *absolute reality* of phenomena. No quality or attribute can be attached to it. However, it can be named, defined and differentiated. The name Suchness is yet another falsehood; however, if we do not develop the concept of Suchness and name it, we will not be able to apprehend its true meaning and will not be able to see it even when it is right in front of our eyes.

CHAPTER IV: THE ENLIGHTENMENT PROCESS

In reality, Suchness is just an abstract term. The Masters who developed the Paññā (Wisdom) School of Buddhism used the term Suchness to describe the immutable nature of worldly phenomena that remains as-such (*tathatā*). This term is used to mean that the true nature of all things, or their true essence, is "as such". This essential nature does not change through time or space. It always remains *exactly as such*. As it is that which does not have a name, nothing can be added to or removed from it, it cannot be augmented or reduced, it is not large or small, dirty or clean.

According to the Paññā School, Suchness is a state that can only be attained in wordless awareness, or more precisely in the state of *wordless cognitive awareness* that comes from our Ultimate Cognition faculty. This profound point is the reason why Masters of the Paññā-Paramitā (Perfect Wisdom) School considered Suchness as the ultimate means to attain perfect wisdom. They considered Suchness as the true appearance as well as the ultimate essence of worldly phenomena. The person who successfully becomes one with Suchness will experience the development of his/her spiritual energy.

When we attain the ultimate stage of wordlessness, Suchness is also Non-Suchness *(Atathatā)*. The term Suchness is used to designate the everlasting truth. It has remained the same from the origin of time and continues to be the same now; it remains unchanging through time. Whether the Buddha had come into being or not, the essential nature of phenomena is always *as-such*. The Buddha is the person who has experienced the state of Suchness and taught us the way to experience it and enter the ultimate spiritual path. With this means, we can attain the triple goal of ending suffering, and attaining enlightenment and liberation from birth and death.

Suchness is the true appearance or the immutable appearance of all phenomena. It is the principle that allows the phenomenal world to be in a state of *immobile as such*.

It is only through intuitive wisdom that one can apprehend the meaning of Suchness because Suchness is the reality *such as it actually is* as well as the *non-falseness*. Suchness is a term that can be used to help us end suffering and attain enlightenment and liberation from birth and death, if we know how to become one with it.

Suchness means the *pure essence*. It is the *fundamental nature* and the *basic substratum* of the phenomenal world. It does not have a dualistic appearance, is undifferentiated and cannot be divided because it is rooted in the **Unborn**. This is why Suchness does not abide in anything; it does not have a past, a present, or future; it does not have a differentiating appearance but it still exists like any other reality. Just as we speak about it, it is right there in front of our eyes.

Suchness is a term that is used to name the essential nature, fixed and firm, of all phenomena. It is the ultimate and unconditioned essence of all phenomena. It can be apprehended through spiritual realization, but it is also the condition that leads to complete enlightenment, if the idea of "I" is subsumed into it. We cannot see it through our worldly eyes nor can we find it through the reasoning of the intellect. Nor can we lose it by separating ourselves from it, because it is part of us. It is inside the elements that constitute the five aggregates, but it is not the five aggregates. The practitioner needs to seek it, because s/he needs to dwell in the everlasting *tathā*-mind in order to attain peace in this transient life and open the path to enlightenment, spiritual wisdom, and liberation from birth and death.

6. The doctrine of the Twelve Links of Dependent Origination

Question: Master, could you please explain the Buddhist view of the universe?

Answer: It is the Buddha's view of the universe, which consists of the laws of impermanence and no-self, as well as the characteristics of Change and Transformation, Specific Conditionality, Emptiness, Illusion and Suchness of the phenomenal world.

Question: Master, and what is the Buddhist view of humanity?

Answer: It is the Buddha's view of humanity. Human beings are worldly phenomena, and therefore they are subject to the same laws identified above. In addition, as sentient beings, humans are also subject to the doctrine of the Twelve Links of Dependent Origination, also called the Twelve-Link Chain of Causal Relations.

Question: Master, is the doctrine of the Twelve Links of Dependent Origination part of the doctrine on the Specific-Conditionality-nature of worldly phenomena?

Answer: Yes, it is. According to the suttas, the Buddha realized the law of cause and effect applicable to the cycle of birth and death of human beings over past, present and future.

Question: Master, could you please explain further the Specific-Conditionality-nature of worldly phenomena?

Answer: The discussion on the Specific-Conditionality (*Idappaccayatā*)-nature of phenomena is central to the Law of Dependent Origination. It is a universal law that says that all phenomena are subject to specific conditions. Every phenomenon is influenced by conditions in their interdependent relationships. We need to examine carefully each link in the chain of causality.

Specific Conditionality is often mentioned before Dependent Origination (*Paṭicca-samuppāda*). The two terms have the same meaning. They are both compounded words. Specific Conditionality is the fourth most important characteristic in the Buddhist concept of cause and effect.

A condition or causal relation is defined as a factor, i.e. a phenomenon that must exist together with other phenomena to allow the manifestation of a phenomenon.

A set of conditions (*paccaya-samūha*) such as "Contact causes Feelings and Sensations" means that Contact is the condition that leads to the arising of Feelings and Sensations. Master Buddhagoṣa used the term *paccayuppanna dhamma* to designate a conditionally arisen phenomenon. Therefore Contact is the condition that leads to the conditionally arisen phenomenon Feelings and Sensations. In turn, Feelings and Sensations are the conditions that lead to the conditionally arisen phenomenon Craving. The word *paccaya* in Pāli means a condition or a set of conditions. When it means a set of conditions it refers to the complexity of many conditions coming into consideration. Another Pāli term, *hetu* (meaning cause), is often used in the Nikāya interchangeably with *paccaya* (causal conditions). The Buddha said:

What is dependent origination? Bhikkhus, from a condition, there is arising. Whether there is an arising of Tathāgatas or no arising of Tathāgatas, that element still persists. It is the stableness of the Dhamma (dhammaṭṭhitatā), the fixed course of the Dhamma (dhammaniyāmatā), specific conditionality (idappaccayatā). A Tathāgata awakens to this and breaks through to it. Having done so, he explains it, teaches it, proclaims it, establishes it, discloses it, analyzes it, elucidates it. (Samyuktāgama, "Connected Discourses of the Buddha", SN 12)

From the above text, we can notice two opposing concepts: on the one hand is dependent origination (*paṭiccasamuppāda*) and specific conditionality (*idappaccayatā*), and on the other hand is cessation *(nirodha)* or liberation. These two poles are two fundamental views in Buddhism which are in direct opposition to the theories of Destiny and Non-Destiny. They also stipulate that all worldly phenomena are subject to the law of cause and effect; any event that occurs is the result of one or more events; anything that happens at a specific point in time has its origin in something that happened some time prior to it. By contrast, the Non-Destiny doctrine totally refutes the necessity of the order created by the law of cause and effect.

The Doctrine of Dependent Origination combines the four laws that apply to worldly phenomena. These four laws tell us that worldly phenomena occur through the agency of causal conditions. Anything that is born depends on others. Dependent origination also means that "any given phenomenon does not contain the foundation of itself" or *"idappaccayatā"*. This doctrine teaches us that phenomena occur as a result of causal conditions, and that everything depends on something else.

Question: Master, could you please tell us about the 12 links of dependent origination?

Answer: They are: (1) Ignorance, (2) Mental Formations, (3) Consciousness, (4) Name and Form, (5) Six Senses, (6) Contact, (7) Feelings and Sensations, (8) Craving, (9) Clinging, (10) Existence, (11) Birth, and (12) Aging and Death.

Question: Master, in what suttas can we find the teaching on the Law of Dependent Origination and the Twelve-link Chain of Causal Relations?

Answer: Notably in the Khuddaka Nikāya, "The Minor Discourses of the Buddha", book 3 Udāna ("The Inspired Un-prompted Discourses of the Buddha"), Ud 1.3. In the eighth week, the Buddha sat and contemplated the Law of Dependent Origination over the three watches of the night.

In the first watch of the night, the Buddha realized the Law of Dependent Origination in the forward order:

This being so, that is; from the arising of this, that arises. That is to say: because of ignorance there are mental formations; because of mental formations, there is consciousness; because of consciousness, there is name-and-form; because of name-and-form, there are the six sense bases; because of the six senses bases, there is contact; because of contact, there are feelings and sensations; because of feelings and sensations, there is craving; because of craving, there is clinging; because of clinging, there is existence; because of existence, there is birth; because of birth, there is aging, death, sorrow, lamentation, suffering, grief, and tribulation. And so there is an origination of this whole mass of suffering.

In the second watch of the night, the Buddha realized the Law of Dependent Origination in the reverse order:

This not being so, that is not; from the ceasing of this, that ceases. That is to say: from the complete disappearance and cessation of ignorance, mental formations cease; from the cessation of mental formations, consciousness ceases; from the cessation of consciousness, name-and-form ceases; from the cessation of name-and-form, the six sense bases cease; from the cessation of the six sense bases, contact ceases; from the cessation of contact, feelings and sensations cease; from the cessation of feelings and sensations, craving ceases; from the cessation of craving, clinging ceases; from the cessation of clinging, existence ceases; from the cessation of existence, birth ceases; from the cessation of birth, aging, death, sorrow, lamentation, suffering, grief, and tribulation all cease. And so there is a cessation of this whole mass of suffering.

In the last watch of the night, the Buddha realized the Law of Dependent Origination in both forward and reverse orders:

This being so, that is; from the arising of this, that arises. That is to say: because of ignorance there are mental formations; because of mental formations, there is consciousness; ... because of birth, there is aging, death, sorrow, lamentation, suffering, grief, and tribulation. And so there is an origination of this whole mass of suffering.

This not being so, that is not; from the ceasing of this, that ceases. That is to say: from the complete disappearance and cessation of ignorance, mental formations cease; from the cessation of mental formations, consciousness ceases; ... from the cessation of birth, aging, death, sorrow, lamentation, suffering, grief, and tribulation all cease. And so there is a cessation of this whole mass of suffering.

Question: Master, this is a chain of links that results in the endless cycle of rebirth for human beings. So how can one be liberated from rebirth?

Answer: We can end the cycle of rebirth by cutting any link in the chain.

Question: Master, could you please provide a concrete example?

Answer: We can cut the first link, ignorance, through wisdom. We do so by understanding the universal laws that govern humanity and the universe, such as the laws of impermanence, suffering, no-self, and cause and effect; that the essential nature of phenomena is emptiness, and illusory existence; and that all phenomena have Suchness-nature, which makes them equal. With this insight, we no longer cling tightly to things because we understand that they are ephemeral; we let go of our passion for worldly pleasures; our mind starts to transform; and we develop a new perspective on life. We start our spiritual practice, attain a stable state of samādhi and become one with the states of Suchness Samādhi, or Emptiness Samādhi, or Illusion Samādhi. At this point, we have ended suffering and experience peace and freedom from concern. When causal conditions cease, we will leave this world fully awakened and will not be compelled to be reborn by the force of our karmic consciousness. However, if we wish to return to this world to pursue the Bodhisattva Way and help other beings, we will freely be reborn in accordance with our vow.

CHAPTER IV: THE ENLIGHTENMENT PROCESS

Question: Master, can we find nowadays a sacred vestige in Bodh Gaya that marks the location where Buddha realized the Law of Dependent Origination?

Answer: Yes, there is one. About 25 meters from the Bodhi tree in the northwestern direction, King Aśoka erected a roofless house called the Jewel House (*Ratanaghara*) to commemorate the place where the Buddha sat and contemplated the Law of Dependent Origination.

Jewel House *(Ratanaghara)*

Question: Master, what is the origin of the Buddhist flag?

Answer: Let me tell you the history of the Buddhist flag.

History of the Buddhist flag

A six-color aura was said to have appeared all around the Buddha's body when he sat in contemplation of worldly phenomena and realized the Law of Dependent Origination. The six colors consist of two parts.

- The first five colors emanated from the Buddha's body. They are: (1) blue (*nīla*), (2) yellow (*pīta*), (3) crimson (*lohita*), (4) white (*odāta*), and (5) scarlet (*māñjesṭṭha*)

- The sixth color was a combination of the other five colors into a bright and resplendent (*prabhāsvara*) color that reflects back. This aura is called the six-colored Buddha-ray (*ṣaḍvarṇā-buddha-raśmi* in Sanskrit).

It was not until the 19th century, on April 17th, 1885, that the Sri-Lankan newspaper Sarasavi Sandaresa proposed a Buddhist flag incorporating the six colors. Eleven days later, on the occasion of the *Vaishāka* day (or *Vesak*, or *Vesakha*), Venerable Migettuwatte Gunananda Thera officially hoisted this flag at Dīpaduttarārāma Pagoda in Kotahena. This was the first time the Buddhist flag officially appeared, in Sri Lanka. At the following year's event, on April 8th, 1886, most pagodas and lay Buddhists' houses displayed the Buddhist flag.

Today, the six-color flag has become the official flag of Buddhism around the world.

3

THE SIGNIFICANCE OF

THE BUDDHA'S ENLIGHTENMENT

1. The key to developing our potential for enlightenment: the *tathā*-mind

Question: Master, could you please explain further the process by which the Buddha developed his transcendental wisdom?

Answer: It is the process of attaining the Unborn, or *tathā*-mind. I will summarize this process here.

A vow became reality

After leaving home at the age of 29 and spending six years battling his own mind, Prince Siddhattha Gotama sat down at the foot of the *pipphala* tree and methodically went through four stages of meditation using his own method to finally vanquish his egotistical self and its army of inner demons. He had totally *abandoned* all that was born, comprising the discursive reasoning of the intellect, the pondering of the mind faculty, and the discrimination of the consciousness.

As a result, he attained the Unborn and was liberated from birth, aging, sickness, death, sorrow and defilement.

Question: Master, could you please provide references to the suttas?

Answer: In the Majjhima Nikāya, there is a passage in "The Noble Search" sutta where the Buddha described to his disciples how he realized the Unborn. He said:

Then, Bhikkhus, being myself subject to birth, having understood the danger in what is subject to birth, seeking the unborn supreme security from bondage, Nibbāna, I attained the unborn supreme security from bondage, Nibbāna; being myself subject to aging, having understood the danger in what is subject to aging, seeking the un-aging supreme security from bondage, Nibbāna, I attained the un-aging supreme security from bondage, Nibbāna; being myself subject to sickness, having understood the danger in what is subject to sickness, seeking the un-ailing supreme security from bondage, Nibbāna, I attained the un-ailing supreme security from bondage, Nibbāna; being myself subject to death, having understood the danger in what is subject to death, seeking the deathless supreme security from bondage, Nibbāna, I attained the deathless supreme security from bondage, Nibbāna; being myself subject to sorrow, having understood the danger in what is subject to sorrow, seeking the sorrowless supreme security from bondage, Nibbāna, I attained the sorrowless supreme security from bondage, Nibbāna; being myself subject to defilement, having understood the danger in what is subject to defilement, seeking the undefiled supreme security from bondage, Nibbāna, I attained the undefiled supreme security from bondage, Nibbāna.... (Majjhima Nikāya, "The Middle-Length Discourses of the Buddha", Ariyapariyesanā Sutta, "The Noble Search", MN 26:18).

After six years of hardship, the vow of Prince Siddhattha Gotama finally became reality. He had attained his spiritual realization and the ultimate enlightenment, the Perfect Full

CHAPTER IV: THE ENLIGHTENMENT PROCESS   195

Enlightenment. He became the historical Buddha. He was then 35.

Pipphala Tree

The *pipphala* tree was later renamed *bodhi* tree, or enlightenment tree, to commemorate the fact that the Buddha attained enlightenment when seating under a *pipphala* tree. The place where the Buddha attained enlightenment became a *bodhimaṇḍa*, or "place of enlightenment", a spiritual holy place.

From that time, the story of the Buddha's enlightenment continues to live in the spirit of all those who seek enlightenment and liberation. His model of attaining enlightenment and liberation based on a self-reliant individual practice became entrenched among oriental people, especially among those who practice samādhi meditation. This model of attaining enlightenment and liberation is founded on the state of Immobility Samādhi, or the *tathā*-**mind**, which is the meditation stage in which the Buddha attained enlightenment.

Bodh Gaya, site commemorating the place where the Buddha attained enlightenment

2. Reconfirming the Buddha's realization of the Law of Dependent Origination

The Buddha's comments on the truth that he just realized

After the Buddha realized the Three Insights at the end of the fourth week, he stayed around the Bodhi tree for another seven weeks to contemplate the truths that he had

CHAPTER IV: THE ENLIGHTENMENT PROCESS   197

realized. At the end of the seventh week*, the Buddha recognized that the truth that he had just realized is very profound, subtle, peaceful, sublime, hard to see, hard to understand, and not in accordance with ordinary worldly reasoning, as it goes against the common world view. It would be difficult for ordinary people to understand this truth and only the wise could apprehend it. For this reason, the Buddha was reluctant to teach the *dhamma*, even though it would help free other beings. He thought that living beings have too many desires, are too attached to desires and would not understand the teaching on dependent origination, the law of cause and effect or the Specific-Conditionality-nature of phenomena. It would especially be difficult for people to understand his method of spiritual realization through the immobility of the three mental formation processes. It would be difficult for any person to totally abandon his/her desires.

He considered that it would be a waste of his energy if people could not understand the *dhamma* that he had realized. In "The Noble Search" sutta (*Ariyapariyesanā Sutta*), the Buddha recounted to his disciples the thoughts that he had at the time:

Then, Bhikkhus, I considered: 'This Dhamma that I have attained is profound, hard to see, and hard to understand, peaceful and sublime, unattainable by mere reasoning,

---

* According to the Discipline Basket 1 (*Vinaya-Piṭaka 1*), p. 1, after the Buddha attained enlightenment, he sat in the lotus position at the foot of the Bodhi tree for the first seven days to enjoy the happiness of enlightenment (*Vimutti-Sukha*). During the second week, he stood and looked at the Bodhi tree without blinking. The introductory chapter to the Jātaka Commentary (*Jātaka Nidānakathā*), book 1, p. 77, also mentions that, in the second week, the Buddha stood and looked at the Bodhi tree without blinking. The Commentary on the Dhammapada (*Dhammapadaṭṭhakathā*) (Book IV, p. 71) recorded that the Buddha stayed around the Bodhi tree for seven weeks after attaining enlightenment.

subtle, to be experienced by the wise. But this generation likes desires, rejoices in desires, craves desires. It is hard for such a generation to see the truth, namely, specific conditionality, dependent origination^1. And it is hard to see this truth, namely, the stilling of all mental formations, the relinquishing of all grounds for rebirth^2, the destruction of craving, dispassion, cessation, Nibbāna. If I were to teach the Dhamma, others would not understand me, and this would be wearying and troublesome for me'. (MN 26:19)

At this point, something that he had not experienced before occurred. From inside his Buddha-nature, verses with deep meaning spontaneously sprang up. They indicated that those who still harbor greed and anger would not be able to realize his teaching. For his teaching goes against the greed and anger of the world. It is subtle, hard to realize by the mind of the common people. People who are still deep in ignorance would not be able to understand his teaching. He said:

Thereupon, there came to me spontaneously these stanzas, which were beyond mere comprehension^3 and never heard before:

*How can I teach this Dhamma
That even I found hard to reach;
For it will never be perceived
By those who live in lust and hate.
Those dyed in lust, wrapped in ignorance
Will never discern this abstruse Dhamma
Which goes against the worldly stream,
Subtle, deep, and difficult to see.*
(MN 26:19)

CHAPTER IV: THE ENLIGHTENMENT PROCESS

3. Teaching the *dhamma* according to each person's capacity and the principle of self-reliance in practicing the right method

Question: Master, for what reason did the Buddha eventually decide to teach the *dhamma* for 45 years?

Answer: The Buddha decided to teach people *according to their spiritual capacity*.

Recognizing that the truth that he had realized goes against the worldly flow of desires and does not accord with the perspective of ordinary human beings, he was reluctant to teach.

At that moment, Brahmā Sahampati who dwelt in the Heaven world and knew of his thinking, appeared and pleaded with him to teach. The Buddha agreed to his request.

With his Buddha's vision and his infinite compassion towards all living beings, he was able to know intimately each person's opinions and tendencies, and the level of their spiritual energy. He thought that he would teach to each person according to his/her character and capacity for comprehension. To those with a low capacity for comprehension, he would teach the low level truths, to those with a middle capacity for comprehension, he would teach the middle level truths and to those with a high capacity for comprehension, he would teach the most profound and marvelous aspects of the truths that he had realized[4] and the stages of samādhi that he had experienced.

He recognized that human beings, even though they are all born and live in this world, have different levels of spiritual capacity due to their past karma and the environment in which they live. Some are clever, intelligent, judicious, while others are ignorant, naive, dull; some are kind and others are cruel; some are easy to teach and others are hard to teach. Just as in a pond of blue, pink and white lotus, while all plants grow in the same pond, some could not emerge from the surface, others could reach the surface and yet others could grow high above the surface, untouched by the water.

So he decided to throw the gates to deathlessness wide open and actively teach anyone who decided to abandon their old erroneous beliefs and listen to his teaching according to their spiritual capacity. He said:

Then, Bhikkhus, I listened to the Brahmā's pleading, and out of compassion for beings, I surveyed the world with the eye of a Buddha. Surveying the world with the eye of a Buddha, I saw beings with little dust in their eyes and with much dust in their eyes, with keen faculties and dull faculties, with good qualities and bad qualities, easy to teach and hard to teach, and a few others who knew the danger of being reborn in another world and the danger of committing unwholesome acts. Just as in a pond of blue or red or white lotuses, some lotuses that are born and grow in the water thrive immersed in the water without rising out of it, and some other lotuses that are born and grow in the water rest on the water's surface, and some other lotuses that are born and grow in the water rise out of the water and stand clear, un-wetted by it; so too, surveying the world with the eye of a Buddha, I saw beings with little dust in their eyes and with much dust in their eyes, with keen faculties and dull faculties, with good qualities and bad qualities, easy to teach and hard to teach, and a few others who knew the danger of being reborn in another world and

CHAPTER IV: THE ENLIGHTENMENT PROCESS

the danger of committing unwholesome acts. Then I replied to Brahmā Sahampati in stanzas:

'Open for them are the doors to the Deathless,
Let those with ears show their faith.
Thinking it would be troublesome, O Brahmā,
I did not speak the Dhamma subtle and sublime'.

Then the Brahmā Sahampati thought 'I have created the opportunity for the Blessed One to teach the Dhamma'. And after paying homage to me, keeping me on the right, he thereupon departed at once. (Majjhima Nikāya, "The Middle-Length Discourses of the Buddha", Ariyapariyesanā Sutta, "The Noble Search", MN 26:21)

Question: Master, who were the Buddha's first disciples?

Answer: I will recount to you the story as it was recorded.

After the Buddha had made his decision to teach, out of compassion and knowing his own experience of *inner realization* and *enlightenment*, the Buddha thought of his two former teachers. He thought of teaching them, for he knew that they were wise, had a tranquil mind, and extensive experience with spiritual practice. They would have the ability to understand the Buddha's ultimate enlightenment through the four characteristics[5] of the Law of Dependent Origination and the beyond-reasoning mind, or immobile mind[6] or *tathā*-mind[7]. However, the devas informed him that his first teacher Āḷāra Kālāma, who taught him the Base-of-Nothingness samādhi, had died seven days earlier, and that his second teacher Uddaka Rāmaputta, who taught him the Neither-Perception-nor-Non-Perception samādhi, had also died just the day before.

Teaching the Dhamma to the five ascetic friends

The Buddha felt regret that his two former teachers did not get the opportunity to hear the right teaching on enlightenment and liberation. He then thought about teaching the five ascetic monks who used to practice with him. Using the power of his Buddha's vision, he saw that they were staying at the Deer Park at Isipatana, near Vārāṇasī. A short time later, the Buddha arrived at the Deer Park to meet them.

In order to overturn the five ascetics' erroneous views about the extreme self-mortification practice, the nature of reality, worldly phenomena, their own bodies, and the path toward enlightenment and the ultimate liberation, the Buddha taught them the Middle Way, the Four Noble Truths and the No-Self Characteristic. Like ripened fruits, the five monks attained spiritual realization[8] once they heard these targeted sermons.

CHAPTER IV: THE ENLIGHTENMENT PROCESS

The first one to attain realization was Koṇḍañña. The Buddha twice congratulated him during his sermon on the Four Noble Truths: *"Koṇḍañña, you have realized, Koṇḍañña, you have realized"* (*"aññasi vata bho Koṇḍañño, aññasi vata bho Koṇḍañño"*).

Due to this realization, Koṇḍañña was later known as Koṇḍañña-who-has-attained-the-highest-wisdom[9] (Añña-Koṇḍañña). Five days later, upon hearing the No-Self Characteristic sutta (*anatta-lakkhaṇa sutta*), all five attained the state of arahat[10].

Question: Master, could you please explain the most important factors that lead to spiritual realization?

Answer: First we need to be self-reliant in our practice, and second, we must adopt the right method.

Question: Master, what is being self-reliant in practice?

Answer: It means that we must dedicate sufficient time to the practice, using the two main methods of Samādhi (stillness of mind) and Paññā (wisdom). We need to practice regularly every day without fail our sitting meditation and our meditation while going through our normal daily activities. We do not rely on prayers or help from anyone. This is consistent with the Buddha's teaching in the Mahā-Parinibbāna sutta, "The Discourse on the Great Emancipation": *"we need to light our own torch to see the way, only relying on ourselves and not on others."* (Dīgha Nikāya, "The Long Discourses of the Buddha", DN 16)

Question: Master, why is choosing the right method the second condition?

Answer: The right practice method is like a road that will lead us to our desired destination. This is of utmost importance. Also in the Mahā-Parinibbāna sutta, the Buddha earnestly reminded his disciples to *choose the right dhamma as teacher*. The right *dhamma* is the Suchness (*Tathatā*) method, which enabled the Buddha to attain the state of Supreme Perfect Full Enlightenment. This is why he called himself *Tathāgata*, which means "Such-gone / Thus-come". Later, Mahayanists gave the title of *Tathāgata* to all Buddhas from the worlds of all the ten directions.

Question: Master, could you please explain the meaning of the word *Tathāgata*?

Answer: As the Buddha attained enlightenment while in his Suchness state or *tathā*-mind, he called himself "One who has come as such" (*Tathāgata*). The word *tathāgata* is a compound word that consists of two words: (1) *tathā*, which is an adjective meaning "as such", and (2) *gata*, which is the past participle of the verb *gam* meaning "to go toward", and therefore *gata* means "has come".

4. A revolutionary view of human life: liberating the mind from the oppression of divinity

Question: Master, is it correct that the Law of Dependent Origination is an eternal truth that always exists regardless of whether the Buddha had come into being?

Answer: This is correct. However, the moment when the Buddha realized and proclaimed the Law of Dependent Origination marked a revolution in human thinking that still persists to this day.

Question: Master, could you please explain further?

Answer: Before the Buddha's time, there were many schools of thought in India which offered differing views on the origin of human beings and where they go after death, and on the origin of the universe, its evolution and ultimate end. For example:

- The **Eternalism** theory views human beings as having an everlasting and unchanging soul or Self. This Self emanates from the power of a supreme deity, or God or Brahmā, who created or projected it. After death, the Self will return to the supreme deity for eternity. Similarly, the universe was created by the deity and is everlasting. This theory is also known as the Determinism theory.

- The **Annihilationism** theory takes the view that there is nothing after the end of a human life. There is no karma, no cause and effect, and no life after this one. This is also the Non-Determinism theory.

- The **No-Causality** theory considers that all worldly phenomena, including humans, are created by chance and not by any causal conditions.

After realizing the Law of Dependent Origination and the Law of Dependently Arisen Phenomena, the Buddha saw that human beings and the universe are created from a great number of causes and conditions, and therefore change continuously as these causes and conditions change. For this reason, there is nothing that can be construed as an everlasting and permanent "self" either of a human or the universe. The Buddha proclaimed that the laws of No-Self, or absence of real substance, Change and Transformation and Cause and Effect govern the universe and human life. This means that there is no divine intervention in the creation or evolution of the universe and human life.

Therefore, we can say that the Law of Dependent Origination marks a revolution in human thinking which has liberated the human mind from the oppression of divinity.

5. The message of equality and the abolition of social stratification

Question: Master, what other influences did the Buddha's realizations have on Indian society at the time?

Answer: Indian society at the time was subdivided into castes in accordance with *Brahmin* traditions that had existed before the time of the Buddha.

1. The Brahman caste consisted of priests who held power over spiritual matters and performed religious rites. They believed that they were noble people who originated from Brahmā's mouth and exercised spiritual leadership on behalf of Brahmā. For this reason, they considered that they had the right to be worshipped and lead the happiest of lives.

2. The Kshastriya caste consisted of warriors who believed that they originated from the arms of Brahmā and exercised temporal power on behalf of Brahmā.

3. The Vaisya caste consisted of merchants who believed that they originated from the thighs of Brahmā and held responsibility over economic matters such as trade, farming, and generating wealth in the community.

4. The Soudra Caste consisted of lowly people and slaves who believed that they originated from the heels of Brahmā and had to endure a life of hard labor at the service of the higher castes.

5. The Pariah caste consisted of the most impoverished people who lived outside the fringes of society. They were treated by the upper castes as animals and led a life of extreme suffering, shame and darkness.

Each caste had strict rules. People were born into a caste and remained in it forever without any opportunity for advancement. When the Buddha proclaimed the Equality-nature of all human beings, he also enacted it within his community of disciples. All *bhikkhus* and *bhikkhunis* were equal disciples of the Buddha without any distinction arising from the caste they belonged to before renunciation.

6. **Developing human qualities of compassion and wisdom, building harmonious families, secure societies, prosperous nations and a peaceful world**

Question: Master, is it correct that the immediate aim of Buddhism is to serve humanity? If so, what are the outcomes of leading one's life in accordance with Buddhist teachings?

Answer: First of all, we start by following the Buddha's teaching and practice the four methods of Contemplation *(Anupassanā),* Tranquility *(Samatha),* Stillness of Mind *(Samādhi)* and Wisdom *(Paññā).* Over time, our spiritual wisdom will progressively develop, our compassion and loving-kindness toward others will spontaneously strengthen and we will experience improved physical health.

When we make the vow to take refuge in the Buddha, the *dhamma* (teaching) and the *sangha* (monastic Buddhist community), we vow to follow the five precepts of Buddhist laypersons which are: no harming living creatures, no stealing, no sexual misconduct, no false speech and no consumption of intoxicants. If we abide by these five precepts, we will become a good family member and a good model in our role as son or daughter toward our parents, in our role as husband or wife and in our role as parents toward our children. This will create harmony and happiness in our family.

If there are many such harmonious and happy families in the community then current and future generations will form a secure society, a prosperous nation and ultimately a peaceful world. Peace in the world will be achieved when people have enough compassion, loving-kindness and wisdom to live harmoniously together. The Buddha's teaching will remain relevant as long as there is human suffering. And as long as violence, oppression and wars are still around, the Buddha's message of compassion, loving-kindness and wisdom will need to be transmitted and disseminated to all.

4

CONCLUSION

After his enlightenment, the Buddha continued for over 45 years to teach the *dhamma* to all beings in accordance with their individual capacity[11] and by teaching two levels of truth: the conventional truth[12] and the ultimate truth[13]. At the age of 80, the Buddha passed from this world. Before his passing, the Buddha left to his disciples his last and most invaluable teaching, as recorded in the Dīgha Nikāya, "The Long Discourses of the Buddha", Mahā-Parinibbāna Sutta, "The Discourse on the Great Emancipation", DN 16.

To this day, although societies and human psychology may have changed over time, the teaching of the Buddha remains a torch that guides the way to every successive generation. This teaching provides invaluable guidance to all those with a scientific mind who wish to improve themselves and serve others. It helps them first to develop the spiritual energy that lies within their body, mind and spiritual wisdom, and then to encourage others to follow the spiritual path that the Buddha himself travelled.

Buddhist meditation is still practiced today in many countries in accordance with four major schools: Theravāda, Vipassanā, Developmental and Zen Buddhism. The practice methods of these schools may differ but their goal remains the same. It is to attain *freedom from suffering*, *enlightenment* and *self-liberation*.

THE END

210 CHAPTER IV: THE ENLIGHTENMENT PROCESS

REFERENCES

FOR CHAPTER IV

SUTTAS

1. Kinh Trung Bộ (Majjhima Nikāya) – Translated into Vietnamese by Hòa Thượng Thích Minh Châu, Saigon, 1986, Book 1, pp. 373-379

2. Kinh Tương Ưng Bộ (Samyutta Nikāya) – Translated into Vietnamese by Hòa Thượng Thích Minh Châu, Saigon, 1993, pp. 51-52

3. Kinh Tiểu Bộ (Khuddaka Nikāya) – Translated into Vietnamese by Hòa Thượng Thích Minh Châu, Saigon, 1999, pp. 115-118

4. Kinh Tạp A Hàm (Samyuktāgama), SĀ 12

5. The Middle Length Discourses of the Buddha – A New Translation of the Majjhima Nikāya – Translated by Bhikkhu Ñāṇamoli and Bhikkhu Bodhi, Wisdom Publications, Boston, 1995. Sutta # 26 Ariyapariyesanā, "The Noble Search", MN 26:18, MN 26:19, MN 26:21

6. The Connected Discourses of the Buddha – A new Translation of the Samyutta Nikāya – Translated by Bhikkhu Bodhi, Wisdom Publications, Boston, 2000. Nidānasamyutta, "Connected Discourses on Causation" SN 12:20, "Conditions"

7. Khuddaka Nikāya, "The Minor Discourses of the Buddha, book 3 Udāna, "The Inspired Un-prompted Discourses of the Buddha", translated by Bhikkhu Ānandajoti from the Buddha Jayanthi Tripitaka text, version 2.2, revised February 2008, Ud 1.3

NOTES

NOTES TO THE INTRODUCTION

(P): Pāli, (S): Sanskrit, (V): Vietnamese

1. Inner talk: P: *vitakka*, V: *tầm*. The main meanings of the original Pāli term are: pondering, reflection, reasoning, argumentation, thinking. The real nature of this mental activity is the **self-talk** that occurs in our mind, arising from **us talking to ourselves about a certain topic**.

2. Inner dialogue: P: *vicāra*, V: *tứ*. The original meanings of the Pāli term are: examination, investigation, discursive thinking, deliberation. The real nature of this mental activity is **an inner dialogue that occurs in our mind**, arising from the back and forth discussion that we have with ourselves about the topic that we are contemplating or examining.

The inner talk and inner dialogue processes are prime obstacles for the practitioner of samādhi meditation. In order to vanquish or control the verbal chatter in our mind, we need to *silence* the inner talk and inner dialogue by giving the order "stop verbal chatter". This is how we train our neurons to develop a new habit, the habit of silence.

3. Samādhi without inner talk and inner dialogue: from the Pāli terms *avitakka* (V: *không tầm*) meaning "non reasoning and judgment" and *avicāra* (V: *không tứ*) meaning "non discursive thinking". The core meaning of this expression is the absence of silent verbal chatter. Samādhi without inner talk and inner dialogue is the state of mind when all verbal chatter, muttering, or back and forth discussion in our mind are silent.

4. Feelings and sensations: P: *vedanā*, V: *cảm thọ*, or *thọ*. They are the second group (or "aggregate", P: *khandha*, S:

skandha, V: *uẩn*) that makes up a human body and mind and are also a prime obstacle to the spiritual practitioner. When we are in control of our feelings and sensations, our self-awareness nature will emerge. We will then be able to experience "right awareness", a transformation of our mind, and a body and mind that are in harmony. Going further, we will be able to experience the higher levels of samādhi such as Emptiness Samādhi, Signless Samādhi and Wishless Samādhi. All forms of samādhi are based on the ability to control feelings and sensations. Only when the Feelings and Sensations aggregate is silent will the other aggregates down the chain – Perception, Mental Formations and Consciousness – become silent.

5. Unified mind: P: *cetaso-ekodhibhāva* (P), V: *tâm thuần nhất* (V). This is the state of mind in which the consciousness, intellect and mind faculty are all absent, with only wordless awareness being present. The unified mind is the foundation of all samādhi processes in Early Buddhism, in which the control of feelings and sensations plays a primordial role.

6. Equanimity: P: *upekkhā*, S: *upekṣā*, V: *xả*. The main meanings of the term is "equanimity, indifference, tranquility", but it also means "abandonment, detachment". The Pāli/Sanskrit term has three original meanings: (1) equilibrium, balance (S: *samatā*), (2) a tranquil flow of awareness (S: *prasathatā*), and (3) effortlessness of mind (S: *anābobhogatā*)

The two mental states that cause a loss of mental equilibrium are the states of mental depression, or discouragement and mental exaltation, or exhilaration. When these two states occur regularly, we will not be able to experience equanimity. For the ordinary person, the states of mental depression and mental exaltation occur frequently. For example, we feel depressed when we encounter something that makes us dissatisfied, and feel exalted when we encounter something that satisfies our mind. The mind of the ordinary person never dwells in the state of equanimity. Consequently, depression and exaltation represent the false mind, whereas equanimity represents the true mind.

When we practice meditation and make an effort to concentrate on an object, we will not be able to experience the tranquil flow of awareness (*prasathatā*) and will not attain equanimity. Thus, equanimity also means "effortlessness". This is the stage in which the practitioner has mastered "inner talk and inner dialogue" (or attained the state of "**no talk**") while being totally relaxed and free from the influence of feelings of elation and bliss. This stage follows the long period of assiduous practice to control the speech formation and thought formation processes.

7. **Samādhi aggregate**, or stillness mass, P: *samādhikkhandha*, V: định uẩn. The Pāli term means "the aggregate of stability of full awareness". This is the state of stable stillness of mind with clear awareness of the external and internal environment without any inner talk, inner dialogue, or mental factors arising. The body does not experience any tiredness, the mind does not experience any agitation, the self and consciousness are absent, and there only remains a clear and very stable flow of cognitive awareness. The main effect of the samādhi aggregate is the elimination of mental defilements while bringing the body and mind into harmony and fostering the development of spiritual wisdom. The Samādhi aggregate is founded upon the immobility of mind, or the *tathā*-mind.

NOTES TO CHAPTER I

Section 1

(P): Pāli, (S): Sanskrit, (V): Vietnamese

1. Worldly life: V: *đời sống phàm tục*. This is the life of ordinary people, busy with daily activities focused on interactions between the individual and other people or the environment, or generally speaking between the individual and objects. The vast majority of these activities continuously impact on the five senses and the mind organ, and as a result the intellect and consciousness, or more broadly speaking the worldly mind, is never tranquil and pure. Topics that people have to wrestle with in their worldly life include: thinking, pondering, strategizing, planning, dealing with events, guarding against unpropitious events, love, jealousy, anger, hatred, worry, fear, struggling, perversion, etc. The opposite of a worldly life is a holy life or a life of renunciation. This is the life of people who are truly engaged on the path to self-enlightenment and self-liberation.

2. Worldly sensuous pleasures: V: *dục lạc thế gian*: the passions and pleasures that attract the senses. Worldly sensuous pleasures generally include material objects of luxury, magnificence, lasciviousness, depravation; activities like gambling, addiction, unrestrained enjoyment of food and perfumes; and more broadly all things that attract and entertain the eyes, ears, nose, tongue and body. The human mind becomes addicted to these worldly sensuous pleasures and will find it difficult to abandon them. They are the causes that lead to the formation of mental defilements and old habits.

3. The Born: V: *Cái Bị Sanh*. This term refers to any mental event that is born due to an object. For example, a perception, feeling, sensation, thinking, pondering, differentiating, wanting, worry or sorrow, etc. arises in our mind as our senses come into contact with an object. These mental events would not have arisen if the object had not come into contact with one of the five senses or the mind organ. Therefore they are said to be born.

Furthermore, all material objects such as houses, cars, television sets, properties, fields, orchards, wife, husband, children, gold, jewelry, etc. are all things that were born. These things do not naturally exist in our life. They exist because we want to possess, create, acquire, build, etc.

4. The Unborn: V: *Cái Vô Sanh*. This term refers to the self-cognitive awareness. This is an awareness that does not depend on an object or on our wanting. It has always been present and permanent in each human being. However, human beings are surrounded by the webs woven by the false mind and are not able to recognize it.

The Unborn does not have any sorrow or suffering, and does not have a Self as subject. Monk Gotama went on the spiritual path to seek the Unborn and be liberated from the cycle of birth and death. He attained this ultimate goal after six years of arduous spiritual practice.

5. Blissfulness, bliss: V: *an lạc*. This term refers to the feeling of happiness that arises from an equanimous mind. The practitioner attains this state of mind by internalizing the teaching of the Buddha, such as understanding the impermanent and no-self nature of all phenomena; or by keeping the six senses detached from the six objects of the senses; or by exercising right speech in all circumstances, which means always speaking the truth, saying words that foster harmony and avoiding words that convey envy, vilification, falsehood, or slander or intent to cause harm. Blissfulness flows from abandoning desires and unwholesome states, or achieving a stable state of samādhi. Another way to achieve blissfulness is by being in control of our chattering mind, i.e. by silencing the verbal chatter that continuously arises in our mind.

6. Spiritual faculty, or natural capacity, or inherent capacity: V: *căn cơ*. This term refers to the spiritual energy or spiritual capacity innate in a person. This capacity depends on the karma of the person.

7. Wordless awareness mind, or nature of awareness: S: *Buddhitā*, V: *Tánh Giác*. This term refers to the primordial awareness of all human beings. It is a tacit, silent, non-referential, and wordless awareness. It is the opposite of the self. The nature of awareness remains the same at the various levels of awareness; however it is distinct from consciousness as it is innate and primordial. It is not created and lies outside the purview of knowing by differentiation of the consciousness, or knowing by the intellect or by the mind faculty. It is also called the "holy mind" (V: *tâm bậc thánh*) in Buddhist literature and the "true mind" (V: *chân tâm*) in Zen Buddhism. It is the capacity for self-awareness of human beings, and consists of three functions: ultimate seeing (V: *tánh thấy*), ultimate hearing (V: *tánh nghe*) and ultimate touch (V: *tánh xúc chạm*).

8. Precious teaching, or precious methods: V: *pháp bảo*. This term refers to the teaching that comes from the Buddha, Buddhist Masters and Zen Buddhist Patriarchs, which has the power to guide the spiritual practitioner toward attaining his/her goals.

9. True characteristic of worldly phenomena, or real mark of all things, or the real nature of all things or worldly phenomena: V: *thực tướng vạn pháp*. Refers to the true appearance or the true nature of all worldly phenomena. According to the Buddha's teaching, the true characteristic of all phenomena is Emptiness. This is because all worldly phenomena are governed by the law of dependent origination, and therefore they do not have their own immutable and specific characteristics. However, they have the same true nature, called Suchness-nature (*tathatā*), which is not subject to the law of dependent origination.

10. Clinging to the reality of the "Self", or clinging to the "I": V: *ngã chấp*. This term refers to the misconception that the "Self" is real and possessions of the "Self" are real, everlasting, and more important than anything else. From this misconception arises the clinging to what we possess, from our body, to our material possessions, our loved ones, our thoughts and our points of view. This is a psychological illness that affects all un-enlightened human beings, all those who have not truly understood the Buddhist teaching of impermanence and no-self, even though they may profess an understanding of Buddhism. Those who cling to the misconception of the reality of the "Self" think that their "Self" is real and nobler and cleverer than the "Self" of all other people. They harbor a sense of superiority, want to be ahead of other people, want to defend their opinions, and want to live for themselves rather than for others. This psychological illness tends to create authoritarianism, stubbornness and blindness when dealing with other people because those afflicted by it do not listen to reason, do not see their own shortcomings, and always focus on other people's shortcomings to criticize and disparage. Those who practice meditation but haven't freed themselves from the clinging-to-the-self illness will not be able to experience an inner tranquility of mind and the presence of their wordless awareness mind in their lives. Stability of mind (*samādhi*) and wisdom (*paññā*) will remain elusive for them.

11. Sensual pleasures of the "Self": V: *ngã dục*. This term refers to the craving of the "Self" for what Buddhism calls the five desires: wealth (and material possessions), beauty of the opposite sex (and sexual love), fame (and social rank, status, and good reputation), food and rest.

12. Pride in the "Self", or ego-conceit: V: *ngã mạn*. This term refers to pride in self and contempt for others, the belief that others are not as intelligent or as wise as oneself. Arrogance and impetuousness are the external signs of such pride in the "Self". This is a psychological illness that affects almost all practitioners and non-practitioners of spirituality, even though they may have had a spiritual realization on the law of impermanence and the non-reality of the "Self". Only when the practitioner has achieved a very robust state of samādhi can s/he be free of this illness, because it is only at that point that mental defilements and old habits, including those of self-pride and conceit, are totally eliminated.

13. Go straight home: V: *về nhà*. This is a Zen Buddhist colloquialism that can have one of four meanings: (1) a practice that aims straight at the wordless awareness mind, (2) being one with the wordless awareness mind, (3) creating the conditions for the wordless awareness mind to emerge, and (4) creating the conditions for the *tathā*-mind to be permanently present.

14. Home of the Unborn: V: *ngôi nhà vô sanh*. This is a Buddhist colloquialism that means the self-cognitive awareness mind.

15. Worldly relationships, or worldly conditions, V: *nhân duyên thế gian*. This term refers to the relationships that a person has with his/her family and with society. In meditation, a large web of worldly relationships make spiritual practice more difficult because they are breeding grounds for **inner talk** and **inner dialogue** to continuously arise.

16. Worldly knowledge: V: *tri kiến thế gian*. This term refers to all forms of worldly knowledge such as knowledge gained from books, magazines, newspapers, television, radio or the Internet. In meditation, worldly knowledge is an obstacle to new practitioners as information and news keep appearing in our mind, making it more difficult to stop wandering thoughts.

NOTES TO CHAPTER I

Section 2

1. Conventional truth, or worldly truth: P: *sammutisacca*, S: *vyavahasatya*, V: *tục đế*. The Pāli/Sanskrit words consist of *saccam* (S: *satya*) meaning "the truth", and *sammuti* (S: *vyavahāra*) meaning "conventional". This term refers to truths that are established by human conventions in regard to the main characteristics, differentiating characteristics and appearance of worldly phenomena. Phenomena have always existed in the universe but without being given a name. Groups of humans have used their own symbols, language and writing to give *names* to phenomena in accordance with how they conceive or imagine their characteristics and appearance, while being unable to see their true nature.

For example, in order to differentiate a thing that has many colors and a fragile appearance that grows from the body of a tree, from another thing that also grows from the body of a tree but has a bigger size, a skin and is edible, humans have given the former the name of "flower" and the latter the name of "fruit". Therefore, "flower" is just a concept to which humans have conventionally attached a name in order to differentiate it from other things. Without the naming conventions, people would not be able to differentiate things. For example, there are many types of flowers in a garden, and humans have formulated conventional names such as orchids, chrysanthemums, roses, carnations, etc. to differentiate them. This naming method gives names to phenomena according to their external appearance.

Let us now suppose that we look inside a phenomenon. If we look at a bunch of flowers in a vase, what really constitutes the appearance of a flower? Can we say that the stem, or the crown, pistil, color, or scent is the flower? None of these factors, taken in isolation, can be called the flower. If we now use an electronic microscope which allows us to see objects just five thousandths of a millimeter (five microns) wide, we will see that the flower is made up of much smaller elements. Physicists have identified particles such as protons, neutrons, electrons, mesons, hadrons and quarks. The smallest particle that makes up the flower may be a quark. But quark is still a name that physicists have conventionally given to this small particle of matter. From the Buddhist viewpoint, the true nature of the quark is without consistence and appearance, it is only *emptiness*. However, within this emptiness, there is an energy source that projects itself and results in the movement of particles such as protons, neutrons, electrons, mesons and hadrons.

In summary, the *conventional truth* is based on human beings seeing the external appearance of things that exist in the universe, and using conventions to give these things names. By giving names to things, communication between members of a human community is facilitated. However humans are unable to see through to the true nature of these things or phenomena.

2. Ultimate truth, or absolute truth, or truth of the highest meaning: P: *paramattha sacca*, S: *patamārtha satya*, V: *chân đế*. It is also called the holy truth, P: *ariyasacca*. This is the truth that comes from seeing through to the true nature of things or worldly phenomena. This true nature is *emptiness*, and worldly phenomena only exist as a result of conditions coming together in accordance with the law of dependent origination.

3. Realization: P: *sacchikaranīyā*, V: *chứng ngộ*. This term refers to seeing a truth very clearly through the mind's eye or by one's potential capacity for enlightenment. This is the outcome of an interpretation by one of the three functions of the wordless awareness mind – ultimate seeing, ultimate hearing and ultimate touch – or by the ultimate cognition capacity of the Buddha-mind.

4. Fully Enlightened One: P: *Sammā-sammabuddha,* V: *Vị Chánh Đẳng Giác* or *Bậc Toàn Giác*. In Buddhism, Sakkamuni (S: *Śākyamuni*, V: *Thích Ca Mâu Ni*) is the only Fully Enlightened being in the current world. He is the one who has attained the *tathā*-mind and subsequently gained the Sixfold Higher Knowledge.

5. Pāli: Language that originated in the northwest of India and was later used in the Magadha kingdom in Eastern India. The Early Buddhist suttas were preserved in Pāli in the Tipiṭaka or "Three Baskets" which consists of the

Discourses Basket (P: *Sutta Piṭaka,* V: *Tạng Kinh),* Disciplines Basket (P: *Vinaya Piṭaka,* V: *Tạng Luật)* and Commentaries Basket (P: *Abhidhamma Piṭaka,* V: *Tạng Luận).* Pāli is currently used as a theological language by Buddhist monks in South Asian countries such as Sri Lanka, Thailand, Cambodia, Laos, and Myanmar. The Pāli Text Society, founded in England in the late 19th century, has romanized the writing of the Pāli language.

6. **Sanskrit:** Language used in the suttas and commentaries by the Developmental Buddhism (previously known as Mahāyāna Buddhism) schools.

7. **Southern School**, or Southern Sect, V: *Nam Tông.* This branch of Buddhism originated from the Theravāda school (School of Elders) and uses the Pāli language as reference. It was initially based in Northern India but did not survive the Muslim conquests of Northern India from the 10th century during which Buddhist temples were destroyed and Buddhist monks killed. Hinduism was subsequently established as the state religion in India, and Buddhism never recovered.

Fortunately, Buddhism reached the small island of Sri Lanka in Southern India approximately 300 years after the death of the Buddha, and over many generations became firmly established to form what is called the Southern School. Buddhism eventually spread and became the state religion in a number of countries such as Sri Lanka, Myanmar, Thailand, Cambodia and Laos.

From the beginning of the Common Era, the Theravāda school was disparagingly called Hīnayāna (Smaller Vehicle) Buddhism. Since 25 May 1950, the World Fellowship of Buddhists has adopted the name Theravāda

Buddhism for all Buddhist schools that follow the Hīnayāna tradition.

8. Northern School, or Northern Sect, or Mahāyāna Buddhism: V: *Bắc Tông*. It was formed between 300 years and 700 years after the death of the Buddha and spread from Northern India into Kashmir, Afghanistan, Nepal, Tibet, Mongolia, and China and from there to North East Asia and South East Asia including Japan, Korea, and Vietnam. Mahāyāna Buddhism has today spread to the Western world, to countries such as Great Britain, France, Germany and the United States. Mahāyāna Buddhism is now officially called Developmental Buddhism (V: *Phật Giáo Phát Triển*). It uses the Sanskrit Buddhist texts as reference.

9. Developmental Buddhism: V: *Phật Giáo Phát Triển*. This is the school of Buddhism that was formed between 300 years and 700 years after the death of the Buddha and was previously called Mahāyāna Buddhism. The Sixth Buddhist Council held in 1954-1956 in Rangoon (now Yangon), capital of Burma (now Myanmar), decided to adopt the names Developmental Buddhism and Theravāda Buddhism instead of Mahāyāna Buddhism and Hīnayāna Buddhism respectively.

10. Supermundane powers of the Buddha.

I. The Three Insights: V: *Tam Minh*. See the note below on the Sixfold Higher Knowledge.

II. The Sixfold Higher Knowledge: P: *chaḷ-abhiññā*, V: *Lục Thông*. Also called the sixfold intuitive knowledge (V: *trực giác trí*) or the six supernormal intuitions (V: *siêu trực giác trí*) or the six magical powers (P: *iddhi-vidha*, V: *thần thông*).

In Buddhism, *abhiññā* refers to intuitive knowledge, or the ability to see straight into the true nature of phenomena. This knowledge originates from the wordless awareness mind through the state of samādhi, and is not formed through learning or the highest level of consciousness. Knowledge that is formed through learning is based on discursive thinking by the intellect, or logical reasoning, or differentiation by the consciousness. It is a composite knowledge that is gathered from many sources. By contrast, supernormal intuition is based on the silent mind. The deeper the silence in the mind, the stronger the supernormal intuition will be. Supernormal intuition flows from spiritual realization (P: *sacchikātabhā*) and full realization (P: *abhisamaya*).

The Buddha attained full realization when he realized the Three Insights. The Three Insights were later considered part of the Sixfold Higher Knowledge. The three forms of Higher Knowledge that mirror the Three Insights are:

i. **Higher Knowledge of Own Past Lives**: P: *pubenivāsānussati-ñāṇa* (knowledge of one's own former births), V: *Túc Mạng Thông*.

ii. **Higher Knowledge of Divine Vision**: P: *dibbacakkhu* (clairvoyance or knowledge of disappearance and reappearance of other beings), V: *Thiên Nhãn Thông*. Also referred to as P: *cutūpapāta-ñāṇa*: knowledge of the passing away and rebirth of other beings.

iii. **Higher Knowledge of the Termination of Mental Defilements**: P: *āsavakkhaya-ñāṇa* (knowledge that achieves the total eradication of all addictions or taints; knowledge of the destruction of the taints), V: *Lậu Tận Thông*.

The other three forms of Higher Knowledge are:

iv. **Higher Knowledge of Moving Anywhere at Will**: P: *iddhividhi* (psychic power or psychokinesis, e.g. assuming multiple forms, moving objects through will power, etc.), V: *Thần Túc Thông*.

v. **Higher Knowledge of Divine Hearing**: P: *dibbasota* (clairaudience or divine ear), V: *Thiên Nhĩ Thông*. The Buddha had the ability to hear and understand the language of deities and humans, from any distance.

vi. **Higher Knowledge of Thoughts of Others**: P: *cetopariya-ñāṇa* (telepathic knowledge or penetration into the thoughts of others), V: *Tha Tâm Thông*.

III. The Tenfold Knowledge-Powers, or the ten supernormal powers of the Buddha: P: *dasabala*, V: *Thập Lực*. These ten types of knowledge increase the power of those who possess them, and hence are called "knowledge-powers". The Tenfold Knowledge-Powers of the Buddha are listed in the Majjhima Nikāya, "The Middle Length Discourses of the Buddha", Mahāsīhanāda Sutta, "The Greater Discourse on the Lion's Roar", MN 12:9 to MN12:21, as follows:

i. **Knowledge of what is reasonable or what is not, or knowledge of truth and error**: P: *ṭhānaṭṭhāna-ñāṇa*. This is the knowledge of what is possible and what is not possible in regard to an object or an event by analyzing it in accordance with the law of cause and effect.

ii. **Knowledge of actions and their results**: P: *kamma-vipāka-ñāṇā*, or knowledge of the different varieties of karma and their consequences, P: *kamantaraṃ* *vipākantaraṃ jānāti*. With this knowledge, the Buddha understood very clearly the essence of life and why people experience suffering. He then used this knowledge to instruct his disciples on ways to absolve themselves from their past karma.

iii. **Knowledge of how beings are led to all forms of existence**: P: *sabbattha-gāminī-patipāda-ñāṇa*. With this knowledge, the Buddha knew exactly the characteristics, state, level of happiness, etc. of each being, depending on their karma. (This knowledge is similar to the second one).

iv. **Knowledge of the world with its various and diverse elements**: P: *anekadhātu-nānādhātu-loka-ñāṇa*.

v. **Knowledge of the different dispositions of beings**: P: *sattānaṃ nānādhimuttikatā ñāṇa*.

vi. **Knowledge of the higher or lower state of spiritual faculties of beings**: P: *parasattānam-indriyaparopariyatta ñāṇa*.

vii. **Knowledge of the defilements, purification and advantages of each person in regard to meditation, liberation, samādhi, and attainments**: P: *jhāna-vimokkha-samādhi-samāpattīnam-saṅkilesaṃ vodānam vuṭṭhānaṃ ñāṇa*.

viii-ix-x are forms of knowledge that mirror the Three Insights.

Note: The Tenfold Knowledge-Powers include seven knowledge-powers that the Buddha developed after he attained the Three Insights. The Tenfold Knowledge-Powers are clearly identified in the Majjhima Nikāya, "The Middle Length Discourses of the Buddha", Mahāsīhanāda

Sutta, "The Greater Discourse on the Lion's Roar", MN 12:9 to MN12:21.

IV. The Fourfold Fearlessness, or the Fourfold Perfect Self-Confidence, P: *catu-vesārajja*, V: *Tứ Vô Úy*. They are:

i. **Perfect self-confidence in the perfection of the Buddha's enlightenment**: P: *sabhadhammā bhisambodhi-vesārajja*.

ii. **Perfect self-confidence in his total eradication of mental defilements**: P: *sabbāsavakkhyañāṇa-vesārajja*.

iii. **Perfect self-confidence in his exposition of the hindrances of the Path**: P: *antarāyikadhamānam-yathābhūtā-niccita-vyākaraṇa-vesārajja*.

iv. **Perfect self-confidence in the path that the Buddha is teaching to attain the "All Completeness"**: *sabbasampadādhigamāyanesaggika-paṭipadā-tathābhūta-vesārajja*.

References: Majjhima Nikāya, "The Middle Length Discourses of the Buddha", Mahāsīhanāda Sutta, "The Greater Discourse on the Lion's Roar", MN 12:22 to MN12:28.

V. The Five Eyes of the Buddha, V: *Ngũ Nhãn*. Early Buddhist texts (in Pāli) and Developmental Buddhist texts (in Sanskrit) both mention that the Buddha had five "eyes", with discrepancies, however, in regard to the Universal Eye (P: *samanta-cakkhu*, V: *Phổ Nhãn*) and the Dhamma Eye (P: *dhamma-cakkhu*, V: *Pháp Nhãn*). Apart from the first "eye", the Eye of Flesh, the other four "eyes" symbolically refer to insights, or forms of knowledge or transcendental wisdoms of the Buddha. Their function is to see and to know as-they-are all worldly phenomena, including human beings. The five eyes of the Buddha are:

i. **Eye of Flesh**, P: *maṁsa-cakkhu*, V: *Nhục Nhãn*. This is the Buddha's physical eye, which has the capability to see as far as normal human beings.

ii. **Divine Eye**, P: *dibba-cakkhu*, V: *Thiên Nhãn*. This is the same as the second of the Three Insights.

iii. **Dhamma Eye**, P: *dhamma-cakkhu*, V: *Pháp Nhãn*. This is the knowledge by which the Buddha came to realize the law of cause and effect.

Note: The Dhamma Eye in Pāli texts is equivalent to the Eye of Wisdom (*prajñā-cakṣu* in Sanskrit) mentioned in the Mahāvastu, which is a Developmental Buddhist text written in Sanskrit. In the Mahāvastu, the Dhamma Eye (*prajñā-cakṣu*) is listed in the Tenfold Knowledge-Powers of the Buddha.

iv. **Eye of Wisdom**, P: *paññā-cakkhu*, V: *Huệ Nhãn*. This is the wisdom that led to the Buddha's enlightenment and self-liberation, and his discovery of the path that leads to enlightenment and self-liberation which he would use to teach others.

v. **Buddha Eye**, P: *Buddha cakkhu*, V: *Phật Nhãn*. This is the faculty by which the Buddha knows the minds, thoughts, intentions, nature, and spiritual potentialities of beings. For example, the Buddha had (1) knowledge of the higher and lower states of the spiritual faculties of beings, P: *indriyaparopariyatta-ñāṇa*, and (2) knowledge of views and inclinations of beings, P: *āsayānusaya-ñāṇa*.

VI. Universal Eye, P: *samanta-cakkhu*, V: *Phổ Nhãn*. This type of eye is also mentioned in the Pāli texts. It is considered to be the highest seeing faculty of the Buddha; however it is not listed as the sixth "eye" of the Buddha, but as equivalent to the power of omniscience.

VII. Omniscience, or all-knowledge: P: *sabbaññu*, S: *sarvarjña*, also mentioned in Buddhist texts as P: *sabbaññutā-ñāṇa*, S: *sarvākārajñatā*. This term has been translated into Chinese and Vietnamese as *"Nhất Thiết Trí"*, or *"Nhất Thiết Trí Trí"*. This is the knowledge that enables the Buddha to see clearly through all phenomena in the universe. Arahats do not possess this knowledge. However, although the Buddha had the supernatural powers associated with omniscience, he never declared that he had this power, whereas he did confirm that he had attained the Three Insights (Majjhima Nikāya, "The Middle Length Discourses of the Buddha", Tevijjavacchagotta Sutta, "To Vacchagotta on the Threefold True Knowledge", MN 71).

(The Chinese translation of the Mahāvairocana Sūtra translates *sarvajña* into *"nhất thiết trí trí"* (omniscience, the wisdom of all wisdom). In the Laṅkāvatāra Sūtra ("Descent into Laṅkā Discourse"), the Buddha explained to Bodhisattva Mahāmati ("Great Wisdom") the meaning of the word *tathāgata* and acknowledged that he had *sarvajña* (omniscience). The Mahāyāna Sūtralaṅkāra ("The Great Vehicle Discourse Literature") by Venerable Asanga provides a list of 60 knowledge-powers of the Buddha that includes omniscience.)

11. The Enlightened One: P: *Buddha*, V: *người đã giác ngộ*. This is the name given to Gotama Buddha to indicate that he attained the sublime state of human being that cannot be found in any other human being. The quality of this enlightenment is mainly manifested through the two qualities of Great Compassion and Great Wisdom. His Great Compassion encompasses all beings. After the Buddha attained enlightenment, he traveled ceaselessly for 45 years to teach all groups of human beings as well as deities and Brahmā deities. Through his Great Wisdom, he realized the nature of all worldly phenomena, which include human beings, and knew clearly the origins of sorrow and suffering and the method to terminate them. He was a person who had attained enlightenment and liberation for himself, and then found the way to guide all beings to attain the same enlightenment and liberation. Through the practice of samādhi meditation, he attained transcendental wisdoms such as the Three Insights, the Sixfold Higher Knowledge, the Fourfold Fearlessness, the Tenfold Knowledge-Powers, and the Five Eyes, etc.

12. The Awakened One, V: *người đã tỉnh thức*. This is the name given to Gotama Buddha to indicate that he had awakened from the dream-like state caused by the frantic pursuit of pleasures of the senses that afflicts all of humanity. The Buddha had awakened from this dream and helped others awaken from the same dream. This dream-like state is formed by the misguided pursuit of sensuous pleasures, vacuous honors, temples, palaces, wealth, possessions, and luxury. These things lead only to sorrow and endless rebirth. The Buddha made his awakening tangible through the teaching of contemplation methods, samādhi meditation, and precepts to educate human beings and help them attain the same awakening that he had attained.

13. Transcendental wisdom, or superior wisdom, P: *adhipaññā*, S: *adhiprajñā*, V: *thắng trí*. This term refers to the highest level of teacherless knowledge. According to

Early Buddhism, transcendental wisdom is developed by dwelling in the Unborn, which means the *tathā*-mind or self-cognitive awareness. The term is synonymous with higher wisdom (V: *thượng trí*) which is a combination of higher mind (P: *adhicitta*) and higher discipline (P: *adhisīla*). The higher mind is attained through the practice of contemplation and samādhi, with the aim of developing the energy of self-awareness and not the intellect and consciousness. For this reason, the higher mind is attained by achieving stillness of mind and not by controlling the wandering thoughts that arise in our mind. Only on that basis can transcendental wisdom develop. The practitioner needs to combine higher mind with higher discipline. Higher discipline consists of seriously applying moral precepts in order to keep the mind free from the agitation caused by external causal conditions and help achieve the state of samādhi. In Early Buddhism, transcendental wisdom is developed by applying the Three Practices of Precepts, Samādhi, Wisdom (V: *Tam Học: Giới, Định, Huệ*). If one only focuses on controlling wandering thoughts that arise in the mind, one will not attain transcendental wisdom and will only play a chasing game with wandering thoughts.

14. Self-realization, S: *svāsākshātkar*a, V: *tự chứng*. This term is synonymous with "inner realization" or "inner witness" (S: *pratyak-sākshākara* or *antar-sākshātkriyā*, V: *nội chứng*) and means a realization that one has attained by oneself or a realization that comes from within oneself (inner realization). Self-realization is a fundamental tenet of Buddhist meditation. Practicing meditation without attaining any self-realization is like not being able to "know what hot or cold is like".

15. Mental defilements, P: *āsava*, S: *āsrāva*, V: *lậu hoặc*. This term means etymologically (1) the toxic liquids that seep from plants and flowers, and (2) the pus that seeps from wounds. In Buddhism, it means the toxic elements that lie in the deepest parts of the consciousness and contaminate the mind and cloud the intelligence. They are poisons of the mind. The term *āsava* (mental defilements) is used in Early Buddhist texts and was translated into Chinese/Vietnamese as "*lậu hoặc*". It is synonymous with another Chinese/Vietnamese term "*tập khí*" which is used in Developmental Buddhist texts and literally means "old habits". The term *āsava* has many meanings and designates the passions that affect the human mind and lead to clinging and attachment to worldly sensuous pleasures. There is no exact equivalent in English for the Pāli word *āsava*, which has the following meanings: (1) Taints, or what is spoiled, dirty; (2) Defilement, or the act of making things spoiled, dirty; (3) Corruption; (4) Intoxicants; (5) Infatuations; (6) Addictions; (7) Cankers; (8) Manias; (9) Intoxicating manias.

16. Desires, P: *tāṇhā*, S: *trishṇā*, V: *ái, ái dục, khát ái, khát dục* (other meanings: craving, longing, drought and thirst). This term refers to the demand and craving to satisfy the five senses with something that belongs to one of the five categories of: wealth and possession, sexual lust, fame and status, food and rest. They are the root cause of sorrow and suffering, and the main cause of the endless cycle of rebirth. Desires are the main components of the desire defilement. It is only through a strong state of samādhi or through wisdom – seeing clearly the true nature of all phenomena – that one can hope to eliminate this instinct.

In the doctrine of Dependent Origination (*paṭiccasamuppāda*), Desire and Craving is the eighth link: from

Feelings and Sensations Desires-Craving arise (*vedanā-paccayā-taṇhā*), from Desires-Craving Clinging arises (*taṇhā-paccayā-upādānaṁ*). Desires and craving come into existence through the agency of feelings and sensations. They are a powerful energy originating from instinct and lie deep inside the human mind. They are the main cause for all misfortunes in life.

17. Impermanence, P: *annica*, V: *vô thường*. Impermanence refers to the ephemeral nature of all things in the universe, including concrete objects, thoughts, ideas, perceptions, laws of nature, beliefs and systems of beliefs. Everything changes every fraction of a second; there are no exceptions to this rule. The Law of Impermanence applies to all phenomena. The Buddha realized and proclaimed it as one of the Three Characteristics of Worldly Phenomena (P: *tilakkhaṇa*, S: *tilaksaṇa*, V: *tam pháp ấn*), which are: Impermanence, Suffering and No-Self.

A meditation practitioner who fails to apprehend the impermanent nature of phenomena will have difficulty freeing his/her mind from attachment and clinging to falsehood because s/he continues to see phenomena as real and everlasting. This misconception will lead to resistance to change, subjectivity and authoritarianism.

18. Suffering, P: *dukkha*, V: *khổ*. In Buddhism, the term "*dukkha*" has many meanings: (1) Pain, painful feeling, suffering; (2) Unsatisfactory nature, un-satisfactoriness; (3) Conflict; (4) Disease, illness. For example, if we strongly desire something and put all our hope into getting it, we will suffer if we do not get it. We suffer when people whom we love and respect suddenly depart this world, or experience some calamitous situations. We suffer when a loved one betrays or abandons us. These are situations that make us feel dissatisfied. While this sense of dissatisfaction develops, our mind becomes conflicted. Furthermore, the Buddha called the situation where a practitioner has achieved some results but clings tightly to these achievements and refuses to progress further, an "illness" or suffering.

The Buddha often compares suffering to a vast ocean. His aim when he decided to travel widely and teach the *dhamma* was to guide all human beings out of the sea of suffering. In the Four Noble Truths, suffering is placed as the first truth, called the Truth of Suffering. The Buddha classified suffering into five groups: (1) the four major sufferings of birth, aging, sickness and death; (2) separation from loved and respected ones; (3) Dissatisfaction from not getting what one seeks; (4) Clinging to one's body while it changes from strength to decay is a cause of suffering; (5) Being near, or living with, people, objects and settings that one dislikes also leads to suffering. The path that leads to the elimination of suffering is the Eightfold Noble Path.

19. No-Self, or not-self, non-ego, selflessness, non-substantiality, P: *anattā*, S: *anātman*, V: *vô ngã*. This term means that the "self" does not exist, or does not have a real substance. No-self is identified by the Buddha as one of the Three Characteristics of Worldly Phenomena (P: *tilakkhaṇa*, S: *tilaksaṇa*, V: *tam pháp ấn*), together with impermanence and suffering. The Buddha explained that each worldly phenomenon or unit of material matter, while created, does not have a real substance. This characteristic applies to everything that exists in this world or in the whole universe. Each phenomenon consists of many interdependent elements or causes which come together in accordance with the Law of Dependent Origination encapsulated by the sentence *"this is, because that is"*.

Nothing has a real substance. The Buddha called this characteristic "no-self". Furthermore, in the No-Self Characteristic sutta (P: *Anatta-lakkhaṇa sutta,* V: Kinh Vô Ngã Tướng), the Buddha explained that the human "self" consists in reality of the coming together of five groups, called the Five Aggregates, which are all empty in nature.

20. Knowing things as they are, or knowledge in accordance with reality, knowledge of true reality, knowledge of Suchness, P: *yathābhūta-ñāṇa,* V: *biết như thật.* This term refers to the state of knowing-things-as-they-are without discursive thinking, without inferring, without the involvement of the intellect or the worldly mind (P: *mano,* V: *ý*), where only awareness is present. This state of knowing is a necessary condition for spiritual realization. The term *yathābhūta* appeared in Early Buddhism's Nikāya texts. It means, in relation to events, things and objects of the mind: knowing that they exist if they do exist and knowing that they do not exist if they do not; knowing things exactly as they are, without adding or subtracting anything, and without any conflict in the mind. In the words of the suttas: "Whatever exists, know that it exists; whatever does not exist, know that it does not exist" (*santam vā atthi'ñassati asantam vā natthi'tiñassati*).

In practical terms, when a person is able to know things as they are, his/her wordless awareness mind has emerged because only the wordless awareness mind is able to know things as they are, without adding or subtracting anything. This is referred to as seeing-and-knowing-things-as-they-are or the comprehension of the actual state of things, P: *yathābhūta-ñāṇa-dassana,* V: *như thật tri kiến.*

21. Worldly emotions, V: *phàm tình.* Refer to the common emotions prevalent in a worldly life such as greed, anger, hatred, delusion, pride in self, harboring wrong views, jealousy, suffering from injustice, and vengefulness. The seven commonly listed worldly emotions are: joy/happiness (V: *hỷ, mừng*), anger (V: *nộ, giận*), sorrow (V: *bi, buồn*), fear (V: *úy, sợ*), love (V: *ái, yêu*), hate (V: *ố, ghét*), lust/desire (V: *dục, muốn*). If a meditation practitioner has not developed his/her intuitive wisdom and has not experienced a deep state of samādhi, his/her worldly emotions will seep through and manifest themselves through his/her manners, speech and demeanor. Worldly emotions are fundamentally the result of mental defilements and old habits that were formed in present and past lives when the six senses came into contact with the six objects of the senses. For this reason, worldly emotions can only be transformed or eliminated by the energy of samādhi and insight-wisdom.

22. Clinging to falsehood, V: *vọng chấp*. This term refers to the misconception that falsehood is real, and then clinging to it. It is synonymous with delusion. For example: believing that the body is real and eternal, and not seeing that it is transient and without real substance; believing that rumors are true and not seeing that they may be part of a propaganda campaign maliciously intent on discrediting a person or an organization.

23. Skillful means, or means of success, V: *phương tiện thiện xảo*. This term refers to the special skills and experience of virtuous friends or persons who guide others on their spiritual practice. These skills come from innovative talents of persons who have extensive experience with spiritual practice or who have experienced inner realization. In particular, the Buddha had many skillful means as he possessed magical powers and other supermundane powers such as the Buddha's Eye, the

Wisdom Eye and the Dhamma Eye. For this reason, his listeners easily comprehended the *dhamma* when he taught.

24. Character and temperament, P: *anusāsanī-pāṭihāriya*, V: *tính khí*, a combination of the two words *đặc tính* and *khí chất*. Each person has his/her own character and temperament depending on his/her karma. The Buddha could see clearly the character and temperament of each person, and this is the reason why each person easily comprehended the *dhamma* when he taught.

NOTES TO CHAPTER I

Section 3

1. The 32 special marks of the Buddha

1. Insides of the feet are fleshy and flat.
2. Insides of the feet have a wheel mark, complete with 1000 circles.
3. Toes are slender and long.
4. Fingers are slender and long, like young bamboo shoots.
5. Upper sides of feet are arched and full.
6. Ankle bones are not apparent.
7. Ankle bones are small.
8. Hair on the whole body is pointing upward.
9. Toes and fingers are finely webbed together like the feet of a dominant sparrow.
10. Legs and arms are supple.
11. Skin is soft.
12. Hair on body and on head is curled to the right.
13. Thighs are like those of a dominant stag.
14. Penis is retractable like that of a royal steed.
15. Body is tall and slender.
16. When standing up, hands reach below the knees.

17. Body has a golden hue.
18. Seven body areas are flat and fleshy: hands, feet, shoulders and neck.
19. Upper body is developed like the body of a lion.
20. Jaws are like the jaws of a lion.
21. Spine is erect and regular.
22. Shoulders are level across the neck.
23. Full set of 40 teeth. Teeth are clear, white, small, regular and tightly set.
24. Voice is as pleasant as the sound of a Brahmā deity. Sound of voice is as clear as the cry of the *karavika* (S: *kalaviṅka*) bird.
25. Tongue when stretched can reach the hairline above the brow.
26. Eyelashes are long and broad like those of a dominant bull.
27. Eyes are brilliant and blue.
28. Crown of the head has a fleshy protuberance that is round, regular in shape, with hair curled to the right.
29. There is white hair between the two eyebrows, curling to the right.
30. Lower jaw is like the jaw of a lion.
31. Areas below arm-pits are well filled.
32. Heels are round and pleasant-looking.

2. World Emperor, P: *Rāja Cakkavattin*, V: *Hoàng Đế của thế giới*.

3. Ceremonial Plowing of the Land, V: *Lễ Hạ Điền*.

4. Sandalwood, V: *hương chiên đàn*, or *trầm hương*.

5. Kāsi: city in Central India, nowadays called Benares, and reputed for the production of fine silk.

6. **Under garment**, P: *antaravāsako*, V: *nội y*: cloth worn next to the skin.

7. **Robe,** P: *sanghati*, V: *thượng y*: an external cloth draped over the body.

NOTES TO CHAPTER II

Sections 1 and 2

(P): Pāli, (S): Sanskrit, (V): Vietnamese

1. Holy life, or pure life, P: *brahmacāriya*, V: *phạm hạnh*. This term refers to the pure and tranquil life of a monk or a layperson who has made the vow to voluntarily live in strict accordance with all Buddhist precepts until death. The concept of holy life helps the practitioner abide by the discipline, purify the mind and eventually be free from the demands of the worldly mind, i.e. not being drawn into unwholesome acts and emotions driven by envy, calumny, jealousy, hatred and malice. A holy life helps the meditation practitioner to achieve a samādhi state of mind more easily because the mind is not busy pursuing the objects of the six senses or carried away by society's judgmental entanglements.

2. The Base of Nothingness, P: *Ākiñcañāyatana*, V: *Vô Sở Hữu Xứ*. This term means "the place where nothing exists" and refers to the mental state in which the meditation practitioner experiences nothingness around him/her during and after the sitting meditation session. Under this method, although the practitioner's mind is still and unperturbed by objects, the self and consciousness continue to be in operation because the Base-of-Nothingness samādhi is grounded in the I-consciousness, in which the self (subject) and object are both present. In the practitioner's mind, there is still the dualistic existence of the Base-of-Nothingness phenomenon and the practitioner who wants to achieve this state. In this practice, *wordless awareness* is yet to emerge. It is for this very reason that the Buddha realized that this samādhi method does not lead to freedom from illusion, seclusion from passion or to true cessation, peace, higher knowledge and enlightenment.

3. Neither Perception nor Non-Perception, P: *N'eva saññāyatana*, V: *Phi Tưởng Phi Phi Tưởng*. This term refers to the state of non-perception but also not non-perception, or the state of non-cognition of anything that happens in the environment. In that state, clear awareness is not present. The Buddha realized that this samādhi method, like the previous one, does not lead to freedom from illusion, seclusion from passion, true cessation, peace, higher knowledge and enlightenment. For this reason, he rejected this method of meditation. He subsequently found his own method of meditation that focuses on the Unborn and the unborn wisdom.

4. Yoga meditation: method of meditation founded in India long before the time of the Buddha and later codified by Venerable Patañjali in the Yoga Sutra. In regard to meditation, this method is built on attaining four levels of "formless" samādhi states (*Arupāsamāpati: the four Formless Attainments*). The first level is the Base of Boundless Space (P: *Akāsānañcā-āyatana*, V: *Không Vô Biên Xứ*), the second level is the Base of Boundless Consciousness (P: *Viññānañcāyātana*, V: *Thức Vô Biên Xứ*), the third level is the Base of Nothingness (P: *Ākiñcañāyatana*, V: *Vô Sở Hữu Xứ*), and the fourth level is the Base of Neither Perception nor Non-Perception (P: *N'eva saññāyatana*, V: *Phi Tưởng Phi Phi Tưởng Xứ*).

Before he attained enlightenment, the Buddha had reached the last two levels of Yoga meditation which are the Base-of-Nothingness samādhi state and the Neither-Perception-nor-Non-Perception samādhi state. However, he abandoned

NOTES

these two methods of meditation because they did not help him attain enlightenment and ultimate liberation.

In the Khuddaka Nikāya ("The Minor Discourses of the Buddha"), book 3 Udāna ("The Inspired Un-prompted Discourses of the Buddha"), Ud 8.1, the Buddha said that one needs to go beyond the above-mentioned four levels of meditation in order to attain the immobile mind, or the *tathā*-mind, and to terminate all suffering.

5. Supreme state of sublime peace, V: *vô thượng tối thắng an tịnh đạo lộ*. The Buddha also called this state the Unborn, because the Unborn leads to enlightenment, liberation and the state of *Nibbāna*. In the words of Zen Patriarch Bodhidharma, this is the wordless awareness mind (V: *tánh giác*). The wordless awareness mind consists of four elements: ultimate seeing, ultimate hearing, ultimate touch and ultimate cognition. Of these four elements, ultimate cognition is the one that causes the Buddha-nature to develop. The Buddha attained enlightenment through ultimate cognition. The other three elements of the wordless awareness mind – ultimate seeing, ultimate hearing, and ultimate touch – are all associated with sense organs, whereas ultimate cognition comes into effect when the mind is totally silent.

6. Discipline, V: *luật*: rules of abstinence. These are precepts that are listed in the charter of a religious organization with the aim of helping the practitioner maintain purity of body, speech and thought, and reduce misguided acts that create bad karma and obstacles to the training of the mind. All Buddhist practitioners have a set of rules that they abide by.

7. Wise person, or intelligent person, V: *kẻ có trí*. The Buddha used this term to designate a person who has awakened, has oriented his/her life toward spirituality and experienced samādhi meditation, rather than someone who focuses on following religious faiths, believes in tradition and has not experienced samādhi meditation. The Buddha considered his two former teachers as wise persons.

8. Abide, or dwell, stay, V: *an trú*.

9. I-consciousness, V: *Ta-ý-thức*. This is consciousness with the "self" as the subject, as distinct from self-awareness where the subject is "the Owner", our "own nature", or our "true self". A strong I-consciousness is an obstacle to the meditation practitioner because the mental chatter can never be silenced.

10. Disenchantment, V: *yểm ly*: awakening from the dreamlike life, or the ending of illusions. This term indicates that the Base-of-Nothingness and Neither-Perception-nor-Non-Perception meditation methods are still within the realm of illusions. Illusion is what creates the states of mind that accord with "nothingness" and "neither perception nor non-perception".

11. Dispassion, V: *ly tham*: ending of wanting. This term indicates that the two Base-of-Nothingness and Neither-Perception-nor-Non-Perception meditation methods still involve the practitioner wanting to attain these two states of mind, and therefore is not free from wanting.

12. Cessation, V: *đoạn diệt*: the eradication of all mental defilements which are the causes for the endless cycle of rebirth. This term indicates that the two Base-of-Nothingness and Neither-Perception-nor-Non-Perception meditation methods do not lead to the termination of mental defilements, and hence the endless cycle of rebirth.

13. Peace, V: *an tịnh*. This term indicates that the two Base-of-Nothingness and Neither-Perception-nor-Non-Perception meditation methods do not end agitation in the mind.

14. Higher wisdom, or higher knowledge, insight, understanding, P: *adhipaññā*, V: *thượng trí*. Refers to a special form of knowledge (*ñāṇa*) that involves the energy of cognition (V: *nhận thức*) and wisdom (V: *trí huệ*), and not of the intellect (V: *trí năng*). With higher wisdom, one knows clearly the nature of one's mind and the nature of the phenomenal world. It originates from a stable or deep state of samādhi. The Buddha realized that his higher wisdom had not emerged despite his attaining the two mental states of Base-of-Nothingness and Neither-Perception-nor-Non-Perception. For this reason, he decided to abandon these two meditation methods. "Higher wisdom" is often seen as the combination of "higher mind" (P: *adhicitta*, V: *thượng tâm*) and "higher discipline" (P: *adhisīla*, V: *thượng giới*). It is synonymous with "transcendental wisdom" (P: *adhipaññā*, V: *thắng trí*) (refer to Note #13 to Chapter I – Section 2).

NOTES TO CHAPTER II

Section 3

1. Self-mortification, or austerity, P: *tapo*, V: *khổ hạnh*. Buddhism considers extreme self-mortification practices as misguided. These practices aim at punishing the body and include living naked, living like dogs, cows and other animals, consuming filthy food and water, subjecting oneself to starvation, etc. They may have beneficial results such as vanquishing malicious behaviors and unwholesome states but do not lead to enlightenment and liberation. The

Buddha practiced self-mortification and fully appreciated this fact. For this reason, he taught practicing austerity in the holy way by respecting purity, avoiding extremes, avoiding self-punishment and being without desire for praise, respect or donations. The person who practices pure austerity needs to clearly understand that the aim is to prevent the six senses from being drowned in the search for pleasure. This will enable a sitting meditation practice that trains the mind to: become pure and free from anger, hatred, pride in self, harboring wrong views; suffering from injustice, jealousy, and vengefulness; developing the Four Immeasurable States of *loving-kindness, compassion, sympathetic joy, and equanimity*; and developing wisdom. Once the practitioner has attained a wholesome mind, the practice of austerity is no longer required.

In the Majjhima Nikāya, "The Middle-length Discourses of the Buddha", Devadaha Sutta, MN 101:27 the Buddha said:

A Bhikkhu considers thus: 'What if I exert myself in what is painful?' He exerts himself in what is painful. When he does so, unwholesome states diminish and wholesome states increase. At a later time he does not exert himself in what is painful. Why is that? The purpose for which that Bhikkhu exerted himself in what is painful has been achieved; that is why at a later stage he does not exert himself in what is painful.

In addition, in the Dīrghāgama, "The Long Discourses of the Buddha", Travel Sutra, DA2, the Buddha talked about seven factors that increase the practice of the *dhamma*, and identified "Exertion in austerity" as the fifth factors. In the Majjhima Nikāya, "The Middle-Length Discourses of the Buddha", Mahāsīhanāda Sutta, "The Greater Discourse on the Lion's Roar", MN 12, the Buddha explained clearly the meanings of austerity in accordance with the holy way and inferior austerity, and proclaimed himself a practitioner of austerity. Also in the Dīrghāgama, "The Long Discourses of the Buddha", Sandhana Sutra, DA8, the Buddha explained to lay practitioner Sandhana the differences between tainted austerity and pure austerity, and urged him to follow pure austerity and forgo tainted austerity.

2. Superhuman states, V: *pháp thượng nhân*. Practitioners of self-mortification in ancient India believed that its earnest practice will take them to superhuman states of being that ordinary people cannot attain.

3. Distinction in knowledge and vision, V: *tri kiến thù thắng*: extraordinary capacity for knowledge and vision.

4. Noble wisdom, or wisdom of the holy person, V: *thánh trí tuệ*. Refers to wisdom without attachment. It is equivalent to seeing, hearing and touching things as they are, knowing things as they are and cognizing things as they are. Noble wisdom is founded on the principle of seeing-and-knowing things-as-they-are (V: *như thật tri kiến*).

5. Exertion, or energetic effort, striving, P: *padhāna*, V: *tinh cần*.

6. Vigor, or exertion, fortitude, virility, P: *viriya*, S: *virya*, V: *tinh tấn*. Also means effort, enthusiasm, courage in acceptance, steadfastness. It is the second of the Five Powers (P: *panca balani*, V: *ngũ lực*) that develop with spiritual practice.

7. Tranquility, or calmness, serenity, P: *passaddhi*, S: *prasrabdhi*, V: *khinh an*. Tranquility is identified as one of the Seven Enlightenment Factors (P: *sambojjhanga*, V: *thất giác chi*). It is often described as a pair: tranquility of body

(P: *kāya-passaddhi*, V: *thân khinh an*), and tranquility of mind (P: *citta-passaddhi*, V: *tâm khinh an*). When our intellect is awakened, both body and mind become tranquil. Tranquility of body refers to the silencing of the three aggregates: Feelings and Sensations aggregate (P: *vedanākkhandha*, V: *thọ uẩn*), Perception aggregate (P: *saññakkhandha*, V: *tưởng uẩn*) and Mental Formations aggregate (P: *saṅkhārakkhandha*, V: *hành uẩn*). Tranquility of mind refers to the silencing of the Consciousness aggregate (P: *viññāṇakkhandha*, V: *thức uẩn*).

In other words: (1) when the Consciousness is not activated, the mind is tranquil, and (2) when the three aggregates of Feelings and Sensations, Perception and Mental Formations are silent, the body is tranquil.

These two states are commonly associated with experiencing the state of Full and Clear Awareness (V: *Chánh Niệm Tỉnh Giác*) or awake awareness (V: *tỉnh thức biết*). As a result, the parasympathetic nervous system is activated and releases the biochemical acetylcholine which generates the feeling of tranquility of body and mind in the meditation practitioner.

8. Breathingless meditation, P: *appānaka jhāna*, V: *thiền nín thở*. This is a practice in Yoga meditation.

9. Holy One, V: *Bậc Thánh*: a person who is more talented, more capable and more virtuous than ordinary people.

10. Elation and bliss, P: *pīti-sukham*, V: *hỷ lạc*. This is the state of feeling joyful, energized, and at ease, comfortable. It is a result of practicing the continuous, and wordless or silent, awareness of the breath. In this process, the awareness of the in-breath and out-breath has an effect on two systems:

1. The hypothalamus, which secretes the biochemical dopamine. This biochemical generates a feeling of pleasure, peacefulness, called "bliss" (V: *lạc*), and

2. The parasympathetic nervous system, which secretes at its extremities the biochemical acetylcholine. This biochemical generates the feeling of joy, called "elation" (V: *hỷ*).

Furthermore, when the meditation practitioner attains a deep state of samādhi, i.e. when all mental chattering and mental murmuring have been silenced, dopamine will be secreted by the substantia nigra organ at the top of the brain stem. The substantia nigra has a large reservoir of dopamine.

11. Secluded from desires, or secluded from sensual pleasures, V: *ly dục*. The meditation practitioner needs to forgo all desires of achieving anything during the practice. If s/he harbors a desire to achieve anything, his/her mind will not be silent. The effect of being secluded from sensual pleasures is the control of inner talk (P: *vitakka*, V: *tầm*).

12. Unwholesome states, or evil thoughts, P: *akusala dhamma*, V: *bất thiện pháp*. Greed-desire (V: *tham dục*), anger-hatred (V: *sân hận*) and delusion (V: *si mê*) are the three root causes of evil thoughts and deeds. In order to attain a state of samādhi, the practitioner needs to purify his mind first by avoiding illegal deeds, and not causing sorrow and suffering to others. Only then can the mind of the practitioner be free from anxiety and remorse about what s/he has previously done to others and about other matters. The effect of seclusion from unwholesome states is the control of inner dialogue (P: *vicāra*, V: *tứ*).

The Buddha taught that a fundamental condition for attaining samādhi is the seclusion from desires and unwholesome states. The Buddha remembered that he had entered the state of samādhi when, as a young child, he sat in meditation under the rose-apple tree during the Plowing of the Land ceremony organized by his father, King Suddhodana. Twenty years later, he experienced the same state of mind as when he was a child. His mind was free of all desires. He experimented with the breathing method to see whether he would attain samādhi again. He did experience samādhi, and then asked himself: "Am I afraid of this samādhi state?" Inside his mind came the answer: "No, I am not afraid of it!"

The Buddha then continued with his breathing in and out and experienced tranquility in his mind. He knew then the path that he would need to follow. He saw his feeble and emaciated body and the loss of all its physical strength, and decided that he needed to resume eating normally to recover his health.

When the Buddha sat in meditation under the *pipal* tree, he applied again the breathing method that he had experienced in his youth, and entered samādhi immediately.

Later, the Buddha identified seclusion from desires and unwholesome states as conditions for entering the first samādhi stage. This means that by not wanting to achieve anything when we sit in meditation, we will achieve what we want to achieve. Therefore, in this instance, the Buddha had raised the intention of "No talk" to achieve the state of seclusion from all desires and unwholesome states. "Seclusion from desires" and "seclusion from unwholesome deeds" does not mean that one must have achieved the abandonment of all desires, evil thoughts and deeds before starting the practice of samādhi meditation, as some commentators have said.

When we guide our meditation students in their practice towards the first samādhi state, we have interpreted the meaning of "seclusion from desires and unwholesome states" by asking students to say softly the two words "No..Talk..", just enough for them to hear, for several days. This will lead them to experience the first samādhi state.

13. Condensed cognition, V: *nhận thức cô đọng*. This term refers to cognition about a subject that has been, through repeated practice, condensed into a single-thought awareness in the mind. This allows the subject to be apprehended as an image in the mind without any word arising in the mind. Condensed cognition is the foundation for non-dualistic awareness of a subject. It apprehends the subject exactly as it is, in its entirety, without any detailed thinking or reasoning occurring in the mind.

14. Rose-apple tree, P: *jambu*, V: *cây mận đỏ, cây diêm phù đề*.

15. First meditation, V: *thiền thứ nhất, sơ thiền*. This is the first of four meditation stages that the Buddha gradually experienced after he abandoned the self-mortification practice. The first meditation stage generates a feeling of elation and bliss (V: *hỷ lạc*) based on seclusion from all worldly desires, evil thoughts and through applying the method of awareness of the in-breath and out-breath. When the practitioner abides in the first meditation, his/her mind is yet to be unified because inner talk and inner dialogue are still present. The practitioner voluntarily raises inner talk and engages in inner dialogue on the topic of breathing. In this process, mental chatter still automatically arises.

16. With inner talk and inner dialogue (P: *savitakka savicāra*, V: *có tầm có tứ*).

With inner talk (P: *savitakka*, S: *savitarka*, V: *có tầm*): with pondering, reflection, reasoning, inner chatter of the mind or verbal thinking.

With inner dialogue (P: *savicāra*, V: *có tứ*): with analytic thinking, discursive thinking, or with silent inner dialogue.

With inner talk and inner dialogue: with thinking and discursive thinking about objects. Here, the object of the inner talk and inner dialogue is the breath, and mentally following and remembering about the length, shortness, depth and shallowness of the in-breath and out-breath. In this instance, inner talk is the raising of a thought about the in-breath and out-breath. Inner dialogue is involved in imagining, observing and analyzing the states of the in-breath and out-breath, i.e. their depth/shallowness and length/shortness.

17. Pleasant feeling, or comfortable feeling, pleasurable feeling, P: *sukha vedanā*, V: *lạc thọ*. This state is achieved by focusing the mind and following the in-breath and out-breath while sitting in meditation with the back upright and not paying attention to surrounding events. During this process, the biochemical dopamine is secreted by the brain stem, generating a feeling of joy and peacefulness in the practitioner.

NOTES TO CHAPTER III

Sections 1 and 2

(P): Pāli, (S): Sanskrit, (V): Vietnamese

1. Bodhi tree, (V: *cây Bồ Đề*): literally means enlightenment tree (*bodhi* means "enlightenment" in Pāli). The Buddha attained enlightenment at the foot of this tree, and this is why this type of tree has been known as *bodhi* tree, or bo tree. This is the *pipphala* tree, also written as *pipal* tree.

2. Supreme enlightenment, V: *giác ngộ tối thượng*: the highest form of enlightenment, the one that leads to liberation from rebirth.

3. Inner serenity with unity of mind, P: *sampasādanam cetaso ekodibhāvam*, V: *nội tĩnh nhất tâm*. This is the state called "unified mind" (P: *cetaso ekodhibhāva*, V: *tâm thuần nhất*) and means a mind in which there is no pondering, reflecting and discursive thinking, and where there is only a non-verbal awareness. This awareness occurs regardless of the existence of objects. The "unified mind" was seen by Buddhist Commentary Masters from some schools of Buddhism as equivalent to the "one-pointed mind" (P: *citassa-ekaggatā*, V: *nhất tâm*).

For this reason, we need to clearly understand the meaning of these two terms. The "unified mind" is a mind in which there is only wordless awareness. It represents the nature of awareness and is also called the wordless awareness mind (V: *tánh giác*) and single-thought awareness (V: *đơn niệm biết*). This is a complete awareness of the environment or an object while the mind is in a pure and clear state. This awareness does not have a subject (who is being aware) and an object (of the awareness). However it has subjectivity because it exists by itself. In order to reflect this subjectivity, Developmental Buddhist and Zen Buddhist Masters have associated it with a hypothetical subject by calling it "the Owner", or "the true nature", or "the true self".

The state of samādhi is founded upon the unified mind. The person who is accustomed to using the intellect, consciousness and mind faculty will not readily be able to experience the unified mind. This is because the intellect, consciousness and mind faculty are aspects of knowing that make a distinction between self and others; are based on language; have a subject who knows and an object being known; and have the urge to report. In this process, the mind is always agitated and is attached to opposites.

If we understand the "one-pointed mind" as a way to concentrate on an object, then this mind is not the unified mind. This one-pointed mind is the main obstacle to achieving the state of samādhi because "self and phenomena" will continuously appear in the mind of the practitioner, because s/he needs to use his/her consciousness to concentrate on the topic or the object of meditation.

4. Attention, or attention of the mind, mental activities, P: *manisikāra*, S: *manaskāra*, V: *tác ý*. This term refers to the intention initiated by the self to do something. It is the root cause for the generation of karma, either good or bad karma. It is also an obstacle to attaining the state of samādhi.

5. Wordless awareness, V: *niệm biết không lời*. This term refers to the state of being aware of an object without any accompanying word-thoughts arising with the awareness.

This is awareness through the wordless awareness mind (V: *tánh giác*). It is the opposite of the verbal awareness of the consciousness. Wordless awareness is the foundation of samādhi meditation. Verbal awareness is the foundation of the contemplation (V: *quán*) practice method.

6. Speech formation, or verbal formations of the mind, P: *vācī-saṅkhāra,* V: *ngôn hành*. This term is synonymous with mental chatter (V: *tâm ngôn*), or whispering, muttering in the mind. In order to achieve the silencing of inner talk and inner dialogue, the meditation practitioner needs to be in control of the speech formation function through techniques such as Just Knowing, Silent Awareness, or No Talk in the Mind.

7. Speech area, V: *vùng phát ngôn*. From the 19th century to the end of the 20th century, neuroscientists considered the Broca area to be the speech area. However, in the early 1990s, neuroscientists discovered that the speech area is in fact located in the parietal lobe, while the Broca area is just a decoding area for signals that are transmitted to it through many pathways in the brain.

8. Inner realization, or inner witness, V: *nội chứng*. This term describes a clear realization of what is happening inside the body and mind of the meditation practitioner through *awareness*, and not through the *intellect* or the *consciousness*. This refers to an experiential realization that arises inside the meditation practitioner and often occurs through the agency of the senses exciting one of the three functions of the wordless awareness mind – ultimate seeing, ultimate hearing, or ultimate touch. This method of inner realization involves a sensory response, whereas the method of using the mind to excite the ultimate cognition function involves a self-generated response.

9. **Dwell in equanimity**, P: *vihārati-upekkhā*, V: *trú xả*. This term refers to the mind being in a permanent state of equanimity. In this state, one is aware of objects through seeing, hearing, touch, smell and taste but there is not in the mind any thought of liking or disliking, attraction or rejection, regardless of what the object is. This is the result of the third meditation stage, where the wordless awareness mind (V: *tánh giác*) has completely emerged. At this point, the practitioner knows everything clearly while in all four positions (walking, standing, lying, and sitting), without any mental chatter arising in the mind. The six perceptual patterns (V: *mô thức tri giác*) cannot affect the wordless awareness mind. When the mind is in this state, the Feelings and Sensations aggregate has the purity of a holy person's Feelings and Sensations.

10. **Full and Clear Awareness,** or total awareness, P: *sati ca sampajañña*, V: *chánh niệm tỉnh giác*. This is the state of clear awareness without any silent talk about what we are doing and how we are progressing. In this awareness, there is a cautious, evaluative and detailed knowledge of the object rather than just a glancing, superficial and general knowledge of it. This is a characteristic of the wordless awareness mind. In this instance, the Pāli word "*sati*" has been translated into Chinese/Vietnamese as "*chánh niệm*" to clearly indicate that it means "awareness" and not "thought". Combined with *sampajañña*, the term means clear, complete awareness of the whole.

11. **Equanimity and awareness,** P: *upekkhā-sati*, V: *xả niệm*. This is the state of a tranquil mind in wordless awareness. This is a result of the third meditation stage.

12. **Dwell in bliss,** or dwell in comfort, V: *lạc trú*. Bliss is a feeling and therefore emanates from the Feelings and

Sensations aggregate. Bliss is a feeling that comes from the body. Dwelling in bliss is being aware through the Feelings and Sensations aggregate of the comfort and tranquility of the body without any mental chatter arising. The Bodhisattva attained this state because he was in full control of inner talk and inner dialogue. The feeling of elation no longer arises and the mind stays in a state of tranquility (*upekkhako*).

13. Six objects of the senses, or six objects of the mind, V: *sáu trần*. This is a Buddhist term that refers to the six categories of objects that are associated with the six sense-organs, or the six categories of objects of the mind. They mirror the six sense-organs and consist of: visual objects, audible objects, odoriferous objects, flavored objects, tactile objects and mental (or cognizable) objects.

14. Six sense-organs, V: *sáu căn*. This is a Buddhist term that refers to the six sense organs: eye, ear, nose, tongue, body and mind.

15. Mental factors, P: *cetasika*, V: *tâm sở*. The Pāli term has also been translated as mental states, or mental actions. It refers to the states of mind that are expressed through spoken words, gestures, or facial expressions and includes all emotions. For example: facial expressions expressing sadness, joy, love, hate, resentfulness, suffering; spoken words conveying malice, bitterness, gentleness, sweetness, anger or hatred. The Buddha considered Feelings and Sensations (V: *thọ*), Perception (V: *tưởng*), thought (V: *tư*), contact (V: *xúc*), attention (V: *tác ý*) to be mental factors.

16. Thought formation, P: *mano-saṅkhāra*, V: *ý hành*. The Pāli term has also been translated as mental conformation, or creation of the mind, or mental function. It refers to the formation of mental events, or the creation of the mind, or the result of activities from the Feelings and Sensations aggregate and the Perception aggregate, which create the network of concepts. For example, the mind misconceives that worldly phenomena are real and becomes attached to them. This leads to struggling, grabbing, and competing to defend self-interests and creates disturbances and distinction between goodness and evil to satisfy the demands of the false mind. Thought formation is the root cause of sorrow and suffering, it is also an obstacle to attaining the state of samādhi.

The thought formation process involves the Feelings and Sensations aggregate and the Perception aggregate (which is where ideas and concepts are generated). During the third meditation stage, the thought formation process becomes immobile. The Feelings and Sensations aggregate and Perception aggregate become inactive. This is not the same as the technique of samādhi by shutting down Feelings and Sensations and Perception because in the third meditation stage, the practitioner maintains a constant and clear awareness. This is what the Buddha called "full and clear awareness".

17. Bodily formation, or bodily actions, P: *kaya-saṅkhāra*, V: *thân hành*. Actions of the body include: (1) behavior, (2) conduct, and (3) deportment in the four positions (walking, standing, lying and sitting).

In meditation, bodily formation is associated with the act of breathing in and out. The term "immobile bodily formation" in the suttas refers to the state in which the breath falls into a pattern of silence of its own volition. This is also called "pure breathing" (V: *tịnh tức*). When in this state, the practitioner experiences a very clear wordless cognitive awareness of the surrounding environment. A machine measuring his/her breath would show a flat line, and a brain wave measuring machine would record a delta wave.

18. Nanyue Huairang, V: *Nam Nhạc Hoài Nhượng*: Chinese Zen Master named Huairang, from Nanyue, 677-744 CE, who was a chaldisciple of Sixth Patriarch Hui Neng and teacher of Mazu Daoyi (709-788 CE).

When they were at the Wisdom temple on Mount Heng (V: *Hoành Nhạc*), Huairang noticed that Daoyi sat in meditation every day. He asked Daoyi:

- Reverend, what is your purpose when you sit in meditation?

Daoyi responded:

- To become a Buddha.

Huairang took a tile, sat in front of Daoyi's hut and started polishing it. Daoyi found this unusual and asked:

- Master, why do you polish this tile?

Huairang replied:

- I am polishing this tile to make a mirror.

Daoyi was surprised:

- How can you make a mirror by polishing a tile?

Huairang asked back:

- How can you become a Buddha by sitting in meditation?

Daoyi was shaken and asked:

- So what should I do?

Huairang replied:

- If an ox pulls a cart and the cart is not moving, should you whip the cart or the ox?

As Daoyi stayed silent, Huairang continued:

- Are you studying the sitting meditation or are you studying to become a Buddha? If you are studying sitting meditation, know that meditation does not involve sitting, or lying. If you are studying to become a Buddha, know that a Buddha does not have a definite appearance. Do not dwell in the *dhamma*, do not hold onto it, do not let go of it. If you sit to become a Buddha, you might as well kill Buddha. If you cling to a sitting position, you miss the main idea.

(Excerpts from *Trung Hoa Chư Thiền Đức Hành Trạng* (Life and Deeds of Chinese Zen Masters), by Zen Master Thích Thanh Từ, Book 1, pp. 26-27)

19. The Three Insights, or Threefold Knowledge, P: *Tivijjā*, S: *Trividyā*, V: *Tam Minh*. This is a Buddhist term that refers to the three forms of knowledge that the Buddha gained when he attained enlightenment. They are: (1) Insight into Own Past Lives (P: *Pubbe-nivāsānussati-ñāṇa*, V: *Túc Mạng Minh*): ability to remember one's own past lives; (2) Insight into the Divine Vision (P: *Cutupata-ñāṇa*, V: *Thiên Nhãn Minh*) or knowledge of the passing away and rebirth of all other beings; (3) Insight into the Termination of Mental Defilements (P: *Āsavakkhaya-ñāṇa*, V: *Lậu Tận Minh*). The Three Insights were later developed into the Sixfold Higher Knowledge of the Buddha (P: *Chaḷ-abhiññā*, V: *Lục Thông*).

20: Watch, P: *yāma*, V: *canh*: a sub-division of a night. The night was usually considered to start at 7pm and finish at 3am or 4am. The ancient Greeks sub-divided the night into three watches, while the ancient Hebrews sub-divided it into four watches. In ancient China, the night was divided into five watches of two modern hours each, with the first watch being from 7pm to 9pm. In ancient India, the night was divided into three watches of three hours each: the first watch (P: *paṭhama-yāma*), the middle watch (P: *majjhima-yāma*) and the last watch (P: *pacchima-yāma*). The first watch went from 7pm to 10pm.

21. Desire defilement, P: *kāmāsava*, V: *dục lậu*. This term refers to the category of mental defilements that originate from the desires and craving of the six senses (the five sense-organs and the mind organ).

22. Craving for Existence defilement, P: *bhavāsava*, V: *hữu lậu*. This term refers to the category of mental defilements that originate from the craving to exist and the craving for conditions of existence in this life and in future lives.

23. Ignorance defilements, P: *avijjāsava*, V: *vô minh lậu*. This term refers to the category of mental defilements that originate from ignorance and lack of clear-headedness. Ignorance is not the lack of worldly knowledge or academic knowledge, but refers to ignorance of the principles of impermanence, un-satisfactoriness and no-self that govern all worldly phenomena. This ignorance causes the mind to be continuously attached to worldly phenomena.

24. Bare cognition of mind, V: *tâm định tĩnh*.

25. Unblemished, V: *không cấu nhiễm*.

26. Malleable, V: *nhu nhuyến*: refers to a mind that is easy to control.

27. Eons of world-destruction, P: *vivaṭṭakappa*, V: *hoại kiếp*. The Pāli term *kappa* (V: *kiếp*) refers to a "fixed" span of life of a human being or of the universe. It is also used as a unit of measure for a cycle in the life of humanity or the universe. The term Eon of World-Destruction refers to a devolving or destructive cycle in the world's life.

28. Eons of world-formation, P: *saṁvaṭṭakappa*, V: *thành kiếp*: refers to a long formative cycle in the world's life.

29. Inferior, V: *hạ liệt*: of low social status.

30. Superior, V: *cao sang*: of high social status.

NOTES TO CHAPTER IV

(P): Pāli, (S): Sanskrit, (V): Vietnamese

1. Law of Dependent Origination, P: *Paṭicca-samuppāda*, V: *Lý Duyên Khởi*. Also referred to as The Twelve-Link Chain of Causal Relations or the Doctrine of Arising from Conditional Causation.

Dependent origination means the arising from a set of conditions that produce an effect. This is the doctrine that states that the creation of any worldly phenomenon depends on a set of conditions. A set of conditions results in the appearance of another phenomenon, which is also called its birth, arising or origination. This principle is innate in every worldly phenomenon. After the Buddha attained enlightenment, he sat on the last day of the eighth week to re-experience the bliss of enlightenment, and realized the Law of Dependent Origination. He subsequently consolidated his findings under the topic "Theory of the Twelve-Link Chain of Causal Relations".

Dependent origination also means that *conditions give rise to other things*. The Buddha called it the Law of Cause and Effect when he explained the law in the context of human lives. He was merely the person who realized the Law of Cause and Effect and reported it to everyone's benefit.

He said: *What is dependent origination? Bhikkhus, from a condition, there is arising. Whether there is an arising of Tathāgatas or no arising of Tathāgatas, that element still persists. It is the stableness of the dhamma (dhammaṭṭhitatā), the fixed course of the dhamma (dhammaniyāmatā), specific conditionality (idappaccayatā). A Tathāgata awakens to this and breaks through to it. Having done so, he explains it, teaches it, proclaims it, establishes it, discloses it, analyzes it, and elucidates it.* (Samyuktāgama, "Connected Discourses of the Buddha", SA 12)

The Law of Dependent Origination stipulates that all worldly phenomena are formed by many interdependent factors or conditions, and no single factor can be considered the original cause. Phenomena are inter-related and interdependent; they combine with each other and rely on each other to exist. The Buddha said that, whether or not he had come into being, the law of dependent origination remains immutable and everlasting in the universe. He said: *"This is, because that is; this arises, because that arises; this is not, because that is not; this ceases, because that ceases".*

2. Grounds for rebirth, or substratum of rebirth, P: *upadhi or upavidhiviveka*, V: *sanh y*. This term refers to the factors that can support rebirth. For example, craving and desires are support for rebirth, and therefore are considered "grounds for rebirth". Relinquishing all grounds for rebirth means that there is no more rebirth. In order to attain this state, the practitioner needs to dwell in the fourth meditation stage, because in this stage, everything is still and at peace.

3. Beyond mere comprehension, V: *bất khả tư nghì*. This term comes from the Pāli *acintiya* (S: *avyākhyeyā-acintiya*) meaning: inconceivable, inexplicable, unintelligible, inexpressible, also from the Sanskrit word *anibhilāpya* meaning "unthinkable", and the Sanskrit word *anirvacaniya* meaning "inexpressible". It is only through wordless cognitive awareness that this reality, which is beyond mere comprehension, can be apprehended.

4. Realization, P: *sacchikiriyā, sacchikaranam, sacchikatabhā*, V: *chứng ngộ*. In Buddhism, this term refers to the realization of something that we have been searching for over a long time but have found the answer more and more elusive the longer we search. And then suddenly, when we are about to give up (meaning that at that moment we are no longer searching), the solution appears right in front of our eyes through the activation of one of the three components of the wordless awareness mind – ultimate seeing, ultimate hearing, or ultimate touch.

Realization occurs through the agency of the eyes, ears or body provided that our intellect is not operating and we are in a situation of impasse.

The Buddha identified four avenues through which a realization can occur: (1) the body (*kaya*), (2) awareness/thought (*sati*), (3) eyes (*cakkhu*) and (4) wisdom (*paññā*).

Realization through the body is triggered by the body touching an object. Realization through awareness/thought is triggered by hearing a sound such as a listening to a sermon, hearing a cry, hearing one's name called, or by reading a sutta, or a commentary etc. Realization through the eyes is triggered by the sight of an object.

Realization through wisdom is different from the other three situations. In this situation, we are not faced with a situation of utter impasse but have been practicing one of two methods: (1) knowing-and-seeing-as-it-is (*yathābhūtam*) whatever is in front of us, or (2) being at one with one of the higher levels of samādhi, e.g. Suchness Samādhi. In this process, the intellect is inactive, as in the other situations. However, this inactivity is not due to an impasse, but is the result of a deliberate action by the practitioner who seeks to excite the potential for enlightenment that lies within our ultimate cognition function. For this reason, attaining realization through wisdom requires the practitioner to be in the state of samādhi on an abstract topic such as Suchness. Realization through wisdom is not the ultimate stage of development of the consciousness, but is the development of the potential for enlightenment that lies within our ultimate cognition function.

One should note that, although the process of knowing-and-seeing-things-as-they-are involves the eyes, it is different from the process of realization through the eyes as it is not sudden and does not involve the intellect being at an impasse. It involves the practitioner using the eyes to look at the object without any inner words arising in his/her mind.

Realization through wisdom is a process of gradual realization (V: *tiệm ngộ*), whereas the other three avenues result in a sudden realization (V: *đốn ngộ*).

5. Four characteristics of the Law of Dependent Origination: (1) Suchness (P: *Tathatā*, V: *Như Tánh*), (2) Indivisibleness (P: *Avitathatā*, V: *Bất Ly Như Tánh*), (3) Identicalness (P: *Anaññathatā*, V: *Bất Dị Tánh*), (4) Specific Conditionality (P: *Idappaccayatā*, V: *Y Duyên Tánh*).

6. Immobile mind, or totally still mind, V: *tâm bất động*. This term refers to the state of wordless cognitive awareness. This state consists of three elements: (1) immobile speech formation (V: *ngôn hành không động*), (2) immobile thought formation (V: *ý hành không động*), and (3) immobile bodily formation (V: *thân hành không động*).

7. Tathā-mind: this is the Suchness-mind, or the immobile mind, or wordless cognitive awareness. It is also referred to as Buddha-nature (P: *buddhatā*).

8. **Spiritual realization**, P: *abhisamaya*, V: *ngộ đạo*: clear realization of the truth.

9. **Highest wisdom**, P: *aññā*, S: *ājñā*, V: *a nhã*. This wisdom is developed through spiritual realization of the truth. It is not the highest level of development of the intellect, but is the result of the development of our potential for enlightenment that lies within our wordless awareness mind and *tathā*-mind, achieved when the intellect is silenced.

10. **Arahat**, P: *arahat, arahant*, S: *arhat, arhanta*, V: *A La Hán*. Literally means "the perfect one", or "the worthy one", or "the perfect understanding", or "a saintly person".

According to Early Buddhism, the Arahat is a spiritual practitioner like any other in the world but is one who has attained the as-is wisdom (*yathābhūta-ñāṇa*) about worldly phenomena, is cleansed of all four categories of mental defilements and will no longer be reborn in any of the six realms. In the days of the Buddha, the Buddha was the only Arahat who had attained the highest level of enlightenment, the Supreme Full Enlightenment (P: *anuttara-sammā-sambodhi*, V: *Vô Thượng Chánh Đẳng Giác*), and possessed the Three Insights and the Sixfold Higher Knowledge through his own efforts without being guided by a Master. His great disciples also attained the state of Arahat, but they did so by following the teaching of the Buddha and may still have some minor shortcomings. For example, *Moggallāna* (S: *Maudgalyāyana*, V: *Mục Kiền Liên*) often fell asleep when he sat in meditation, and this is why the Buddha taught him the eight ways to combat sloth and torpor. After the Buddha attained enlightenment, he helped liberate his five former friends and Yasa, and these were the first six disciples of the Buddha who became Arahat.

11. Teaching to people's capacity, V: *đối cơ thuyết pháp*: adapting the teaching to suit the capacity for understanding of the listener, and to respond to their needs and requests.

12. Conventional truth: refer to Note 1 to Chapter I, Section 2.

13. Ultimate truth: refer to Note 2 to Chapter I, Section 2.

BIBLIOGRAPHY

1. **Dictionary of the Pāli Language**, by Robert Caesar Childers – New Delhi, India, 1979.

2. **Pāli-English Dictionary,** by T.W. Rhys Davids William Stede, New Delhi, 1993.

3. **A Sanskrit-English Dictionary**, by M. Monier Williams, New Delhi, 1997.

4. **Encyclopedia of Buddhism**, published by the Government of Si Lanka, 1971. Editor: G.P. Malasasekera, O.B.E.

5. **Buddhist Chinese-Vietnamese Dictionary**, by Kim Cương Tử and Thích Thanh Ninh, Hanoi, 1994.

6. **Concise Buddhist Dictionary for Meditation Practitioners,** by Thích Thông Triệt, to be published.

www.ingramcontent.com/pod-product-compliance
Lightning Source LLC
Chambersburg PA
CBHW070556300426
44113CB00010B/1273